THE IGBO RACE

ORIGIN
&
CONTROVERSIES

IGBO-UKWU CULTURE, A VESTIGIAL FULCRUM FOR A TRUE IGBO HISTORY OF ORIGIN

HUMPHREY KANAYO AKAOLISA

Any writer who attempts to recall from obscurity and oblivion the past ages of an illiterate nation, and to lay before the public even the most elementary sketch of its history, will probably have to contend against the strong prejudice of numerous critics, who are accustomed to refuse belief to whatever is incapable of strictest enquiry.

Heinrich Barth.

First Published 2003

Buckstar Publishers, Nigeria

© **Humphrey Kanayo Akaolisa** 2003
+2348024478189
+2348052668434

ISBN 978-1460974711
1460974719

CONDITIONS OF SALES

Dedication

This profound academic work is affectionately offered to the memory of my father

SIR S. B. OBIKWELU(KSJ)

Acknowledgement

In the tail end of 1995, I was called by my father Sir S.B.Obikwelu and handed over some copies of his unpublished works. According to him, the works were meant for publication in one of the local dailies and was written after he read some publications in the Daily Times in the 80's. Precisely, it was a reply to Uzo Egonu's publication in the Daily Times and other similar works and views on Igbo culture.

These works turned out to be a great insight to me, and the basis on which I built my research. But the greatest inspiration I gained from these works was that of stimulation of thoughts and interest. The consequent excitement had the result of throwing me into a very long and tedious research. I carried on the research in consultation with my father, until, unfortunately on the 8th of September 1997, when he passed on to the great beyond. The work came to a break for a brief period and resumed before the December after I have dealt fully with the shock. This time, it was with a new determination to finish this work and fulfill the dreams of my father.

I appreciate the usefulness of my acquaintance with the books and people that either made a positive or a negative impression on my mind during the development of the work. Over and above all, I see the Divine aid from the conception to the development and conclusion of this work.

Akaolisa KSH

Preface

This work "THE IGBO RACE", I am called upon and privileged to write a preface to is presented at a very opportune time; a time when the Igbo people are conscious of the fact that they have not got a definite account of their origin or source region, a time when they are finding themselves on a cross-road of the so called Igbo history most of which are based on personal formulations that border on the ridiculous.

A common feature of all the histories and write-ups on Igbo is that they all stopped at the point where information grows thin and no attempts were made to investigate further. The starting points are equally hazy, incoherent and far-fetched. That is why we read of such accounts as "the Igbo people came from Egypt and so on. A well-known Igbo professor of history has it that the Igbo people started their Southward movement from the junction of the Niger and Benue Rivers and stopped there.

This work borne out of deep and intensive oral and book research is conclusive in tracing the origin of Igbo -History. The author frankly admitted from the onset that he is very critical of the published works on Igbo History and will be happy over any criticism, which you the reader will make on his views provided that such criticisms are relevant and constructive. In his part one, he dealt on the sources of controversies in Igbo history. This is followed by a prolegomenon on Igbo-Ukwu, Aro and Nri cultures.

What Thurstan Shaw did not raise or even see are x-rayed and to some extent explained. He posited that Igbo-Ukwu bronze stand on a class of its own, having no relationship with any known Bronzes in Nigeria and Africa. He proved that the Eri culture of the 16th century has nothing to do with the 9th century of the Igbo-Ukwu culture. They are not contemporaneous, belonging to different cultural epoch and separated by a period of over nine hundred years.

Indeed a glance through this book will convince you that it is many books in one. Using the historical books of Chinua Achebe, "Arrow of God" and "Things Fall Apart" and many published work on humanity, he brought into focus Igbo Religion, society, politics, Arts and Igbo worldview. This work heralded a new dawn in the research on Igbo History. He has in my humble opinion succeeded more than anybody before in ascribing an original home base for the Igbo people with Igbo-Ukwu as the principal dispersal point.

Finally, this work should be taken for what it is worth- a must for all schools and libraries and lovers of Igbo history. I congratulate Humphrey for his courage to present this wonderful work. A philosopher once defined an author as one who is courageous enough to tell the world in writing how little one knows of a thing. By taking up your pen to challenge him, the whole corpus of human knowledge is increased.

13 February, 1999
C.O.Ike

Foreword

The desire by a people to know their roots is a natural propensity. It is also a propensity which distinguishes human beings from other animals. The desire heightens if those roots are shrouded in age-old myths and speculations and when the people are experiencing identity crises. The Igbo race is a classic case.

The question of Igbo origin is a recurrent one, and goes back to Olaudah Equiano in the 18th century. It gathered momentum in the 20th century with the emergence of a country called Nigeria. There are three principal components to the provenance question of the Igbo. First, from where and how did the Igbo come to be where they are today? Second, what was their primordial nuclear settlement, that is, the locale from where they fanned out to occupy the territory we today call Igboland? Third, which of the Igbo sub-culture groups or communities were the torchbearers of Igbo history and civilization?

These questions have generated substantial volumes of scholarly and, sometimes, not so scholarly outpourings from various quarters. As would be expected, opinions have varied, and the basic question remains unresolved. Two explanatory positions seem to dominate the issue of the provenance of the Igbo, namely, the oriental and the Niger Benue confluence theses. The northern Igbo zone (Akaolisa's Agbaenu) is generally thought to enjoy primacy in the settlement process of Igboland. Almost offhandedly, most writers accept the Nri/Eri sub-group as the torchbearers of Igbo history and civilization.

Existing knowledge of the matter seems to have arrived at a plateau of stagnation by the 1980s. Subsequent contributors to the debate have merely rehashed extant knowledge in fresh verbiage and yet arrived at the same destination as their predecessors. Two reasons explain this impasse. One is the absence of fresh evidence to permit a revisit of the *status quo*. The other is timidity or reluctance of younger people to challenge positions staked by older people assumed to be icons of Igbo studies.

Humphrey Akaolisa has refused to be so "intimidated" and to swallow hook, line and sinker the established viewpoints. To be sure, this book is not *per se* a work of dissent. In some places, the writer's view tallies with existing ones; but not in others. Indeed, the primary aims of this book are two fold. The first is to "trace the truth of Igbo history" and present "the correct, undisputed and logical facts..."about that history in order to dispel existing "false and distorted assertions". The second is to rekindle "a spirit of unity and communality into the people" at present fragmented and to inspire confidence in them amidst a miasma of identity problems. The validity of the above twin aims can hardly be honestly challenged. The extent to which the writer has achieved them is an open question. For his age, Humphrey seems to exhibit a fertile and analytically penetrating mind. This he has brought to bear on this work.

Not everybody will, however, agree with the author's analysis and interpretations. They do not have to. The beauty and strength of history is that it is inherently democratic and is at its best when it is in a broil of intellectual debate. And Akaolisa recognizes the inconclusive nature of the Igbo origin's debate, stressing that the motive for his endeavour is not to lay to rest that debate but to open new vistas of inquiry. In this regard, it seems to me that he has been successful. For this book has resurrected and freshened old questions, challenged existing orthodoxies and provoked new lines of inquiry. I recommend it to anybody interested in the subject of Igbo origins and the surrounding controversies.

O. N. NJOKU Professor of History

University of Nigeria Nsukka, 24 February, 2003

Table of Content

Authors Preliminary Notes

1   The Illusory Stage of Igbo History

I once witnessed a bird trying to catch a butterfly in flight. It was a futile chase comprising series of upward, downward and side ward movement. This was due to the inconsistency in the directions of the flight of the butterfly. The inability of the bird to catch the butterfly did not mean that the butterfly did not exist. It is equally mere insanity to dismiss the flight of the butterfly as idiosyncrasy of flight, this being its adaptive feature. This is to say that there is always some kind of order in a seeming disorder. The most important law of order is consistency, which could be consistency in inconsistency.

Series of efforts have been made by different people in different epochs to trace and articulate the history and origin of the Igbo race. Series of anthropological works have also been made on the development of this race. However, one glaring fact about most of the accounts is that they have not been satisfactory. A hasty conclusion that dismisses the Igbo as having no history because of the difficulty in articulating it will be very faulty. This will be an ellipse since for tens, hundreds and even thousands of years, men loved, hated, suffered, invented and fought here as others did elsewhere. "A people without history are not redeemed from time, for history is a pattern of timeless moments" T.S.Eliot. The accounts may not be dismissed as false also, since there are always some elements of truth in every account. The fact about some of the accounts is that they have been carried out about parts or lineages among the race or are only an anthropological research within a period or for an event. These in the whole should require a synthesis.

Again, it will not be an overstatement to say that what Mr. Justice Holmes once called "the inarticulate major premise" of an inherent African (or Negro) inferiority is the master minder of the errors made in most works done on artifacts and works of ingenuity found in Africa. For many years now, whenever anything remarkable or inexplicable has turned up in Africa, whole galaxies of non-African peoples are called to explain it. The Phoenicians, Egyptians, Greeks, Jews, Portuguese are paraded as the inspirers and teachers of those who produced this technology. Besides, African writers or Igbo writers on the race in search of authenticity and the zeal to assert the non-inferiority of the Negroes make claims on oriental origin or influence. They do not just stop here, but attempt to prove their claims by creating linkages.

On the other hand, a lot of anthropological works have been carried out within the past century on the Igbo nation. Significantly, the colonial investigators, which bore the colonial motives, carried out most of these works: the desire to discover efficient methods or means of ruling the Igbo. These works were relevant in the sense that they made an expose of the time and sounded the beginning of documentation of Igbo past. They made the way for greater works on Igbo history and it is on this note that I have wished to make my little contribution to this research. I will begin therefore, with a preliminary exposition that will keep my reader abreast of my view about history and the Igbo race.

2 Ancillary Exposition

There are two ways from which we could look at history. History- by which we mean, the whole corpus of knowledge of the past of man and history, which mean the written record of the past. The history of the Igbo, unlike the history of Europe and America, cannot be discussed in the second sense since there is no written tradition among the early Igbo. Rather, in this work, I shall limit myself to the first sense, that is, the whole corpus of knowledge of the past of man. This is the kind of history we obtain almost exclusively by means of archeology and the evidence provided by such kindred disciplines as folklore, oral tradition, genealogy, physical anthropology (including serology and study of fossils) and other sciences capable of helping us, such as geology, botany, paleontology, pale zoology, philology and ethnology etc. this is not to rule out references to prior useful works already made by people in this domain.

Again, when we speak of culture, people tend immediately to think of all the arts, beliefs and social institutions etc that are characteristic of a community, race etc. In this work however, we are going to take culture at the level of understanding as evidence of intellectual development (of art, science etc) in human society. Igbo-Ukwu culture is evidence of development of some great works of art in Igboland by the Igbo people. This archeological artifact dates back before the 9th century.

Unfortunately, not much have been done on these artifacts with the view of interpreting history from them, rather people spent time trying to claim this culture while others prefer leaving it to putrefy. These artifacts have long been established by anthropologists, historians and archeologists as aspects of Igbo-Ukwu culture and no other. However, I only wish to make it clear here that when I speak of the Igbo-Ukwu culture, I do not speak of arts, beliefs or social institutions in Igbo-Ukwu town or anything in reference to the Igbo-Ukwu people as a town but a culture that unites the whole Igbo aboriginals or simply the proto-Igbo. Perhaps providence has given these artifacts to Igbo-Ukwu, perhaps not, but this is not a matter of concern to me in this work, the usefulness of them being prior in my mind.

Before I step into the work, it must not be forgotten that the further we go back to history, the thinner the records become. It is not unnatural also that the early historians painfully copying by hand all the records of war and dynasties, religious persecution or conservations, migrations and revolutions could not afford the time to describe the chamber pots of the time or the hosiery. Likewise is history based on oral tradition, like that upon which I am to base my research. With every passage of time, little details are dropped. For instance, the early parts of the Christian Bible were passed through oral traditions because of the absence of written tradition up till the time of Solomon when writing was introduced. Because of the wide range of time, therefore, the record was bound to be thin. That is why one can easily see a lot of lapses in the early parts of the Bible, especially concerning chronological order of events and people. But most significantly, this is not in any way termed an error, since this is obtainable in every history that of the Igbo is not an exception. It is clear that whatever remains of the knowledge of such records is never absolutely false. It is on this premise that this work is based, though not without effort to sieve out ideas that are controvertible. Such folklores, genealogies, cultures etc. as left by our fore fathers always contain in themselves some elements of truth to reveal the past. Some fragmented knowledge also remains of the ancient history of Africa. The question after this should then be how best to arrange such artifacts to come to the truest chronological order and include the widest range of true information.

This history may be vestigial in essence. References to other work done by people in the domain may be important and useful but it may be ridiculous building on them without thorough assessment of their findings and proper application of the dialectics of thought.

3 Intellectual Admissions

My late father began this attempt and I wish to bring it to a conclusion. In my convictions, I may be wrong, but if I am proved wrong, may I please be put into the same bag with false historians to which many historians on the Igbo history have fallen. According to Joseph Conrad, "the world is not interested in the motives of an overt act but in its consequences; man may smile and smile but he is not an investigating animal". I wish therefore to express in this pristine copy that my motive is simply to correct the mistakes, improving on the views of my predecessors in the process. Some of my predecessors were in a better position than I to judge the situations provided by particular events, so I am duly bound to accept their views.

In the words of Strauss, 'anyone can become an ethnographer and go out to share the life of a particular society which interests him, but not even the historians, or archeologist can have any personal contact with a vanished civilization; all his knowledge must be gleaned from writings or from monuments which societies left behind. Besides, we must not forget that other forms of society, of which we can learn nothing, even indirectly, preceded those contemporary societies, which have no knowledge of writing,' like the one we have at hand.

Secondly, like A.J.P Taylor I wrote this book to satisfy my literary and historical curiosity. In the word of the historian, to understand what happened and why they happened. Historians are often wont to changing what happened because they are not in the way they wanted them to be. But the profession's ethic demands that they can do nothing about them but to state the truth, as they are, without worrying whether they "support" or "revise" existing prejudices, a reaction of absolute quietism. Perhaps, I assumed this so innocently, but I have to warn the reader that I did not come to history as a judge neither did I aim specifically at revisionism. The fact is that when someone or a group voluntarily or involuntarily turns the apple cart, and has the cart placed in front of the horse, motion becomes impossible. It becomes necessary that an unbiased work channeled to set the cart and the horse in the proper position be made so as to bring back motion to the apple cart.

On the other hand however, in the words of Engels in modern times, freedom of science is taken to mean that people write on subjects they have not studied or have little knowledge about and proclaim this as the only strictly scientific method. I have said earlier that most writers on Igbo history ended up producing some sub-standard works. This is an infantile disease, which marks, and is inseparable from, the incipient conversion of most African historians and philosophers on African philosophy and is borne, in the African predicament. Some in an attempt to counter the "inarticulate major premise" ended up in producing ideas, which end up in riddles that force the other to pick up his pen. It is not my fault therefore that I have to follow this group into realms where, at best, I can only claim to be a dilettante. As a caution therefore, I chose for the most part of this work to limit myself to putting forward what in my judgment are the correct, undisputed and logical facts in opposition to some of my predecessors' false or distorted assertions. This applies in some instance also to anthropology where even the professional anthropologist is compelled at times to pass beyond his own specialty and encroach on neighboring territory, the territory on which he is very much a semi-initiate. I hope that I shall be granted the same indulgence in respect to minor inexactitude and clumsiness of expression as people show each other in this domain.

For the sake of reaching a wider audience, I have chosen to dampen my language for the rest of this work. I also introduced some pedagogy and didacting on my ideas with some concrete references to Achebe's works "Things Fall Apart" and "Arrow of God". I chose these works for their usefulness as documentaries on the Igbo culture hoping that many people are conversant with the works. The result of these modifications is that the work became lengthy. I also plead your indulgence in going through the volume.

4 Aim

Some people may argue against the usefulness of such a history in this atomic and computer age. I will like to remind this group that the present is what emerged from the past, while the "future is what emerges from the present and will remain tomorrow as well as what will come to replace it." We cannot predict the direction of future development or control it without being able to handle the present by analyzing and understanding it, via the way it has come through.

The Igbo race has been one of the races that have been generally plighted by the historical development of the past. Generally, we speak of the African predicament which Africans themselves have almost been stagnated of initiatives on how to surmount. The nightmare of slavery, the psychological trauma brought about by the contact with the European culture; the idea of the "inarticulate major premise"; the colonial scramble for territory and the partitioning of Africa which pitched nations against nations within "nation"; the religious turmoil that resulted from the absence of enculturation process in the christianizing mission; and particularly with the Igbo race- a disorganization of the traditional, social and political mechanism etc. (this is not to rule out the effects of the failed attempt in a civil war to assert itself). All these militate against the efforts of the Igbo race to rediscover itself and begin a meaningful development.

Secondly, the very nature of the Igbo traditional, social and political mechanism imposes a kind of schism on the entire race. The schismatic nature is felt in the political behavior of the people. In the religious sphere, it is glaring in the explosive proliferation of the Christian religion that came to us initially in two denominations and other crises against traditional beliefs. Socially, we see the disintegration into parts of the Igbo race even to the extent that many now attempt to claim non-Igbo origin even while speaking Igbo language, bearing Igbo names and every aspect of Igbo culture. Writers on the Igbo culture and history also tend to be schismatic in the various disagreements especially as regards the debate about the origin. The struggle developed to the extent that some Igbo elements are disowned in some writings as being Igbo, when claiming a sole culture of aboriginals, which excludes most elements. What is more the result of such mentality, together with the result of some ancient inter society antagonism and the development of resentments among some elements who felt cheated or deprived of protection during the past civil war etc, only carry this schism into its unmitigated stage.

This work amidst trying to trace the truth of Igbo history is channeled towards inciting a spirit of unity and communality into our people, which is only fragmentally present among various clans whereas it stands as a major identity of other African races. It also aims at inciting a meaningful confidence into our people at the face of our predicament. This I set out to do by studying the historical development of this race while posing a position of falsifying the "inarticulate major premise".

5 Plan

This work is generally divided into two parts each with two other sub-divisions and minor subsections. The first division of the first part deals primarily with investigating the schismatic character of the Igbo race, the truth of the historical event that brought changes and the Igbo character as a factor. The second division launches a polemic on the different postulations on Igbo origin with the view of uniting them by a critical overview.

The second part deals in the first division with the "inarticulate major premise" and the impact of archaeological discoveries on our history while the final division is a denouement on the theme, Igbo cultural origin.

PART I

Chapter 1

The Genesis of the Schisms and Controversies in Igbo Culture

The Igbo People

The Igbo, of the many nations in Nigeria, are regarded as one of the three main tribes in Nigeria. This is because of their population and influence. They inhabit the Eastern part of Nigeria and are surrounded by the Igala in the North, the Delta City States in the South and the Efik in the South East. At present, they occupy the seven states of Anambra, Imo, Enugu, Abia, Ebonyi, Delta, Rivers and parts of Akwa-Ibom and Benue.

Within these areas, where the Igbo language is spoken, one may also notice a kind of disparity in dialects and cultures. Definitely, every culture has a spatial and definite geographical distribution of traits, complexes and patterns. This attribute of culture introduces the concept of culture area, which is an anthropological one based on the empirical observation at a given period. Onwuejeogwu defines a cultural area as "a geographical delimitation of areas that have the same dominant and significant culture traits, complexes and pattern. A culture area may have culture centers where the highest frequency of the significant culture traits occur as well as culture margins, where these cultures tend to thin out or overlap with culture traits of another neighboring culture area'. (Onwuejeogwu 1975, p.1)

The Igbo culture area is an area delimitable by an imaginary line running outside the settlement of Agbor, Kwale, Obiaruku, Ebu (West Niger Igbo Areas) Ahoada, Diobu, Umuagbayi (Port-Harcourt area) Arochukwu, Afikpo, Ndinioafu, Isiogo (Abakaliki Areas) and Enugu Ezike (Nsukka Area) and Nzam. This imaginary line encloses an area in which the people not only speak the various dialects of the Igbo language but also share typical and significant common culture traits and patterns up to or above 50%.

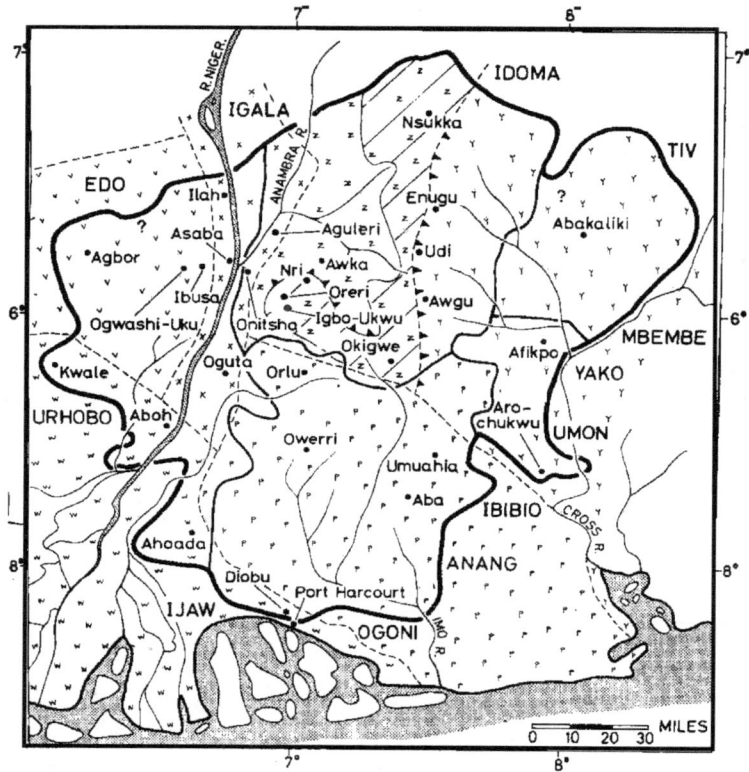

Map of Igbo speaking area, their tribal neighbours and the Cultural divisions.

Different kinds of schism have arisen today among the Igbo, which is mostly coloured by the civil war. Though such schismatic tendencies existed prior to the war or within the Igbo system, it rose tremendously during/since the past civil war in Nigeria, when an Igbo identity is deemed, in many ways, a disadvantage. As a result, many Igbo communities, especially in the present Rivers and Delta States would vigorously deny being Igbo, yet in all intensity, they bear every Igbo culture ranging from the language to the least of all the traits. Prof. B. Nwabueze observed, "Some of the Igbo border communities in Bendel (now Delta) State as well as those in and around Port-Harcourt now strenuously disclaim their Igbo identity. The disclaimer is manifested in practical terms by the latter changing the names of their villages by prefixing them with an 'R' so that Umuokoro becomes Rumokoro.... The intension is to make them not look or sound Igbo names" (Nwabueze, 1985 p.4)

In Delta State, we find the alteration of certain names like Igbo-Uzo (literary meaning "on the way Igbo") being styled to Ibusa or Ibuzo. Most of the people in this area would ridiculously accept that they belong to the culture "Ibo" and not "Igbo" whereas the term 'Ibo' is well known to have originated from the aberrations set on the term Igbo by the Europeans who could not pronounce the alphabet 'gb'. More ridiculously, this same people in the spoken language by typical indigenes would use "Igbo" as the term but only to be found in written form as "Ibo" perhaps perpetrated by the learned few.

That is not all, even east of the Niger, we notice such communities like Onitsha, who have always referred to the hinterland Igbo as Nwa Onyigbo (son of an Igbo). This is a derogatory term, which the Onitsha people used to express in different circumstances their former superiority complex towards the rest of the Igbo people. The Onitsha people cling tenaciously to the oral history of their migration from Benin in the western part of the Niger, perhaps, in an attempt to share in the glory of that well known empire. (Oguejiofor, 1996 p.7). This mentality we know also was exhibited by learned elites like Dr. Nnamdi Azikiwe,

But recent and true anthropological research, done by experts on this area and the area to the west of the River Niger proves them to be in all intense Igbo elements. I will dilate more on this group as the chapter to this work proceeds.

Afigbo described the term Igbo as having shown itself to be rather chameleonic changing meaning according to time and political climate (Afigbo, 1975 p.5). The extent of this schismatic tendency does not end with the border territories or the disclaimers but go beyond into the central Igbo itself. Some parts of the Igbo would regard themselves as superior and not just end there, but regard others as not being Igbo. This is part of the problem people from Abakaliki, Nsukka, and Afikpo etc have to contend with in trying to associate with the rest of the Igbo. It is derogatory for one to be regarded as "Nwa Abakaliki" or "Nwa Nsukka" and generally not a matter of speech but is found in the attitude within their relationships. Just as it is difficult for a non-Igbo to marry an Igbo girl, it is almost as equally difficult for one from Abakaliki to pick a wife from the Agbaenu section of the Igbo culture. Likewise, this attitude permeates all through Igbo culture depending on the extent of disparity in culture and distance.

Community consciousness is deep seated in the Igbo culture and results in a deeper racism within the tribe itself. The Nnewi people, for instance, were said to have told there nearby neighbors Ozubulu, that the wise man in Ozubulu is a fool in Nnewi. Igbo-Ukwu has made similar allusion to Ekwulumiri whereby they would rebuke one who acts stupidly by asking if his mother is from Ekwulu.

This attitude is not just as simple as many have viewed it, it should rather constitute a window in studying this group and worse, in dismissing elements as not belonging to this culture. Such attitude has resulted in the lack of agreement on a common tradition of origin of this people. The schismatic spirit has developed to an extent that each Igbo clan or village group seems to poses a tradition that is peculiar to it. The Onitsha people claim Bini origin and other Western Igbo do the same. The Nri clan has a tradition, which is neatly fitted to the religious hegemony of their people over some section of Igboland and claiming Igala origin. The people occupying the North-East of Igboland claim Ogoja and Ekoi origins and the Aro had a fanciful tale of how their ancestors were part of the Jewish community who were expelled from Spain by Ferdinand and Isabella. The Mbaise will claim that they were created where they exist today (coming from nowhere) and the rest of the Igbo will not accept any of these, both their genealogy and influence as having any part to play in their own development. They will rather split their hairs in attempt to produce their own peculiar history of origin.

Of course, most traditions of origin and migration are usually not more than fairy tales, which lack credibility due to the practical impossibility of providing strong evidence to support them. Just as Isichei rightly pointed out, "the quests for origin rest in an aging historiography for historians are increasingly skeptical about traditions of lengthy migrations in the history of other groups". The inability of oral tradition to hold any water for traditions as lengthy as that of the Igbo, the size of the Igbo speaking element, the absence of a kind of unity among people with common tradition of origin etc may all be as well as pointer to the history and the characteristics of this people.

Of course, within the interior of Africa, there was fragmentation of kingdoms. Apart from the few kingdoms that were brought together by some powerful leaders like the Emperor Menelik II of Ethiopia, Sayyid Said of Zanzibar, Shaka of Zululand and Natals, Moshesh of Bassuto (Lesotho) nations etc, other kingdoms of Africa were fragmented. To the question of this fragmentation, some reasoned that it is because there was abundance of land in Africa and people could therefore migrate and found new kingdoms. Others thought that it was because Africans were more interested in the number of people they were able to rule than in the area of land they acquired. This is unlike the feudal lords of Europe who were interested in the land and property they acquired. This also formed part of the enigmas, which the Europeans had to contend with when they first invaded Igboland. "To start with, the British found Igboland densely populated, but going hand in hand with this dense population was a political situation which baffled and exasperated the average European used to seeing human beings organized in nation states, or at least in the tribal states. The Igbo did not form a state yet by all the rules of the game known to Europeans, they should have formed a state or should have been conquered and incorporated into a state by the one of their neighbors. For one thing, to the west and Northwest, they were flanked by centralized imperialistic and militaristic states, Benin and Idah. It is thought that these states should have partitioned Igboland or the need for self-defense against Benin and Idah should have compelled the Igbo to come together politically and administratively. For another thing, the dense population, squeezed as it was within a very small area of land, should have led to fierce wars for land and therefore to state formation, but neither situation had forced the Igbo to organize themselves into a state on the pattern of Benin and Idah. Instead, each little group of villages remained autonomous and independent, governed by a council of elders presided over by some personage occupying the titular position of either Okpala or Isi Ali or Obi or Eze." (Afigbo 1975 p.14).

A new view of the state of affair in Africa in comparism to that of Europe ought therefore to be sought. But most importantly, a different channel of inquiry may be required for the study of the Igbo race where the spirit of migration and founding of new kingdoms is extreme. A kind of schism that was rare in Africa (The Kikuyu of Kenya seem to be the closest case). This accounts for the much-fragmented Igbo kingdoms and lack of any central command. The reason for this extremity cannot be understood unless we are able to understand the nature of the Igbo man in his political, social and religious life.

The Socio-Political Structure

The Igbo are not only a proud race but also are highly political. They possess an advanced political system when compared with other African ethnic groups. The political system is segmentary. The chief political units are the title group, the age group (elders) priests, and secret societies. Each of these has a part to play in the traditional government of the Igbo. The people are immensely democratic with the result that decisions tend to be slow. Administration is by council whose functions can be legislative, executive and judicial. This is to say that there is no central organization among the whole Igbo and this also accounts for the hegemony of the Aro and the conquest and penetration by the colonial masters. (The hegemony of the Aro is treated in the second chapter.)

The Igbo are so fragmented that just one or more lineages made a clan. The lineages made up of smaller socio-political units. The basic socio-political unit is the Umunna, which is patrilineal. The Umunna may be made up of a number of extended families of family groups. The large families are in turn made up of a large number of nuclear families. The Umunna is headed by the Okpala, but with limited political power. He exercises control with other elders of the Umunna as a kind of primus inter pares in matters relating to the Umunna. In general, clan meetings or affairs, he acts as a representative for his Umunna. Usually, he may not interfere with other activities involving the smaller units within the Umunna unless he is invited to use his influence.

Most of the Igbo clans are heterogeneous while a few clans dwelling along the Anambra River claim to be homogenous. In all, a group of Umunna forms a village section (Ogbe) or a village itself. An aggregate of villages in turn constitutes a town or what in time is called an autonomous community. There are many such clans in Igboland and they are to a large extent independent of one another. A number of clans with the same dialect make up a cultural area. Some of such areas are Awka, Nsukka, Owerri, Onitsha and Abakaliki. The extent of deviation in dialect depends on the extent of external influence. The clan heads are essentially important personages in the political structure of the Igbo. Prestige could be achieved by wealth and good service like when we look at the prestige and honour acquired by Okonkwo in "Things Fall Apart", at a youthful age. The highest qualification for a political post however, particularly for the council of the elders is age.

Government administration proceeds through the council. There are two main councils, the council of elders and the general council of all the citizens called 'Ama-ala' or oha obodo. The council of elders is the highest authority in town. It is composed of the representatives of the major segment heads of the lineages. The elders are looked upon as the fathers of the clan and are expected to protect the interest of the town. A clan has pieces of lands in different locations and the elders have to protect the boundaries of the locations. However, it does not only take age to belong to the council of elders, it also requires some form of good reasoning and wisdom, strength in war and farm work.

The council of elders also legislates on matters of land ownership, cultivation of crops, animal rearing, initiation ceremonies, supply of labour for communal work and marriage customs. Legislation consists of rules to preserve the tradition, check offences and avoid offending the ancestors. No taxes are imposed and the only source of income remains the fines imposed in forms of kegs of palm wine, goats, fowls, sheep and confiscation of other properties. The masquerade group carries out the function of enforcing the law and maintaining peace and order. Among the executive members, we have the priest and the elders. The priests are highly respected and feared because they are believed to be chosen by the gods. Their functions are mainly religious and to some extent political. They offer sacrifice for the people at festivals and they also beat drums for political gatherings and they announce the day of general assembly. A spectacular example of such a priestly role is the function of Ezeulu, the chief priest of Ulu as recorded by Achebe in his work "Arrow of God". The office is not hereditary in most cases and the custodian is believed to be inspired.

At the council, one of the elders may be regarded as the senior political officer or the chairman. Any one of them could be delegated to deal directly with the elders of another clan council. Any one of them could be authorized by the council to be the speaker on a specific issue or to deliver the verdict or the opinion of the council to the general assembly. Usually, other elders will stand behind the speaker to show support and sponsorship. Any member could as well be selected to function as emissary or to carry the council message to other councils in other clans. Just as the case in "Arrow of God", where Akukalia was selected by the people of Umuaro as the emissary to carry their message to Okperi people which turned out to be the crisis among the leaders of Umuaro.

Although the council does not sit without the citizens, it generally sits in public and the people might have a voice. Any man however, could sit with the elders particularly in matters that affect him personally. This measure is a check on the elders. Apart from that, if an individual is dissatisfied with the decision of the council, he could summon the general assembly of the citizens to express his views. If an unpopular decision was taken or if the elders are despotic, the general assembly is called and the citizens could bring the whole business of the town to a standstill through boycott. In "Things Fall Apart", the 'Egwugwu' is the highest and final court of appeal. In chapter 10, we see the dispensation of justice among traditional clans as in the case of Uzowulu versus his wife. There are no lawyers and there are no liars. Judgment is based on true evidence. There is no play with legal technicalities. The Egwugwu is nevertheless a council of the elders under the cover of the masquerade cult. Okonkwo, for instance, as an Egwugwu, became an ancestral spirit. Nevertheless, his transparent nature is against the spirit of the court since the mask is meant to conceal the judges. Such practice eliminates favoritism; bribery and corruption, hence preserve justice.

Women (umuada) are also a powerful group. They can call the general assembly when they feel that the council or the men are neglecting certain things, which they ought not to neglect. The general assembly is normally called for cerebrations, sacrifices, announcements, hearing individual or group complaints and for development programmes.

The elders of the extended families, minor segments or the full council settle disputes. The settlement by the head of the extended families can be regarded as settlement in low court. The case goes from the plaintiff to the headman. He contacts the defendant and both appear on the appointed day, usually in the evening. The case may end here with or without fines imposed on the guilty party. If either of the parties feels dissatisfied with the settlement, the case would proceed to the high court.

The council of elders is the highest court of appeal. Cases reach it through the heads of the families or from individuals or group of people involved. Here the plaintiff and the defendant must appear if necessary with their witnesses. The elders may use age groups as messengers who carry the summons to the defendant. The major offences comprise theft, rioting, land disputes, irregular land lease, and neglect of agreements, obligations and divorces. The people are called together by the aid of town criers.

Land disputes dominate the list of cases. Agreements are not written and sealed as they are done nowadays. Agreements are oral and sealed with palm wine oblations, (and in most cases are honoured). On the other hand, such an agreement may lead to confusion and the resultant dispute will be referred to the council of elders. Here, both parties usually appear with their witnesses (ndi-osiali) and "lawyers" (ndi okaikpe). Witnesses are those who are present when the agreements are contracted and lawyers are the elders who are the keepers of history. An elder may also take a relation of his who is a noted orator to the council of elders, to represent his views where this elder does not see himself as capable of doing so.

The attributes of a good "lawyer" are good memory, good delivery and good reputation. A good use of the precepts, proverbs and traditions would be the base of technical argument. Decisions at all levels are expected to be unanimous and as a result are not taken in haste. The fine to be imposed will depend on the gravity of the offence. Fines are paid in terms of wine, goats, fowls or sheep. In Achebe's "Arrow of God", one sees a very practical example of a council session. When, in the first chapter, we saw the dispute on war policy making, which issued between Ezeulu and Nwaka. Both men were powerful and influential speakers, Ezeulu had to recline on his reputation and his position as the chief priest to convince the people to his principles while Nwaka depended on his skills as a demagogue to take the people along with him. In situations where it is difficult to arrive at a solution, the meeting usually resorts to (Igba-Izu), taking council. A group of five to ten men selected at random at the suggestion of an influential elder. They withdraw from the group and discuss the pros and cons of the issue at hand. It takes a unanimous decision and return to present their decision and the reason, which informed them.

In extremely difficult cases, resort are made to the oracle and quite unlike the modern society, the gods are greatly feared and respected because of their impartial verdict and ability to inflict instant punishment on the defaulter which often come in the form of death. Oracles are shrines at which appeals are made to a god. Priest who acted as the god's mouthpiece issued the god's judgment or opinion. This is done after clients have made offerings to the god. Igbo oracles secure blessings from the gods, fortune or message from the ancestors and pronounced judgment on disputes.

Some of the Igbo oracles became nationally renowned for their impartial verdicts. They include the 'Agballa' oracle of Awka, the 'Igweke-Ala' oracle of Umunnoha, the 'Amadioha' oracle of Ozuzu and the most famous of all the 'Ibini Ukpabi' or long juju oracle at Arochukwu. It is believed that the farther the oracle is from the disputants, the more chance there is for an impartial verdict. In fact, this is why the main oracles at the main lands of the Igboland are disregarded and never received much general recognition. Such oracles include the 'Udo', the 'Ogwugwu' and the 'Idemili'. The effectiveness and therefore the fame of an oracle lay in its apparent ability to kill by supernatural means those disobeying its verdict. Generally, such supernaturally caused death takes the form of a lingering illness, which is put down to disobedience against the oracle. A vivid example of such act by the gods is recorded in the "Arrow of God" when Ezeulu lost his most beloved son, Obika at a time when everybody in Umuaro believed that Ezeulu was not acting according to the will of his god, Ulu. They, therefore, saw the death as the god having taken sides with them and as a punishment to Ezeulu.

Oracles are also effective in killing disputants who invoke it falsely or who knowing the truth, swear to the veracity of their false claims. A litigant who invokes an oracle falsely is believed to be the guilty party, such offenders are at times killed instantly by the oracle and such is the operation of the 'Ibini Ukpabi' oracle of Arochukwu, which made it very famous. On the whole, litigants are so convinced of a famous oracle's powers that they would tell the truth; the final result being that innocence and guilt were correctly apportioned.

On the whole, therefore, the function of the traditional government of the Igbo can be reasonably said to be legislative, executive, judiciary and religious. It provided good administration and organization to carry out its business and organised system of law and justice. It is a useful pattern of government, which provided a system connected with the peoples' religious beliefs, their relationship with one another and their business. The government is simply Theo-centric. It keeps the members of the clan together and makes it possible to call the people a community and not merely a gathering of individuals. It provided leadership.

It is necessary at this point to modify the impression that this account of Igbo traditional government might have so far given that the different clans are absolutely independent of one another. They are not really independent. Many clans are exogamous, which means that men must marry from outside the clan. Thus, one clan was bound to all the surrounding clans by inter marriage. Age grades tend to undermine the independence of a clan because people of the same age over a number of clans may hold more loyalty to their age groups than to their clans. A good masquerade or dance is repeated in different clans as a mark of respect or a goodwill visit to the clan's heads or other clans may deliberately invite the group during festivals or to teach them the dance. The practice tends to unite the clans. Again, wrestling contest, hiring of good drummers, flutters and trumpeters has strong binding effect on the clans, so do secret societies.

The title group also provides bond, which bound different clans together. The 'Ozo' title distinguishes the noble from the commoners and is a qualification for political appointment in a town. The title groups bear different names in different localities such as 'Ozo' for Awka area, 'Ama' for Nsukka area, 'Okpala' 'Eze', 'Nze', 'Ume', 'Obi', 'Dim', 'Ichie' etc. but they bear the same structure. All titled men are therefore politicians and may be popular or unpopular in the council of elders. They could be used politically to test the popularity of the council. The massive attendance and cheering of the people shows approval of the actions of the council of elders and serves as a vote of confidence. Poor attendance will dictate a vote of no confidence and a demand for a change or resignation. However, resignation is not easily obtainable and when such is not achieved, it has often led to dispersion. "Every man should go to become king in his own house".

The political and social culture of the Igbo society can be practically understood by an in-depth study of the novels "Things Fall Apart" and "Arrow of God" written by Chinua Achebe. The books especially "Arrow of God" are not just novels but are also documentaries, which give an account of the Igbo traditional political system and the agent of change and dispersion in the Igbo society. The Igbo generally resist any trait of central leadership or dictatorship. They resist anything that tends to undermine traditional confidence and shake the sense of common purpose and solidarity, which constitute the spirit of traditionalism. Every culture also naturally resists external political influence but that of the Igbo is peculiar for its extremity. This was illustrated during the colonial era, where it was extremely difficult for the colonialist to amalgamate and rule the Igbo kingdom and other similarly organised societies of the Southern Nigeria. The Igbo fought tooth and nail to resist such influences and when the war waged against such traits failed, the Igbo believed on the other hand that "when the roof and walls of a house fall in, the ceiling is not left standing". Everything would have fallen apart and every man retire to his tent i.e. dispersion. This is the typical result of the crisis in "Things Fall Apart" and "Arrow of God". Igbo hardly agree on one point and this had been the bane of Igbo politics and general Igbo socialism.

Igbo Society and Politics in Arrow of God

As arbiter of dispersion in Igbo Culture

(A good part of this section is taken from the work 'Human Dimension of History in Arrow of God, Perspectives on Chinua Achebe' written by Obiechina E.)

In Arrow of God, according to Obiechina, the conflict in the book developed around Ezeulu, the chief priest of Ulu, who is the ritual and religious leader of Umuaro. On the one hand, there is the conflict between the local British administrator, represented by the old administrator, Captain Winterbottom and the native authority represented by the Chief Priest (resisting external influence). On the other hand, there are the internal politics of Umuaro, and the conflicts between the supporters of the Chief Priest and those of his rival, Idemili (resisting dominance or dictatorship). On another level belongs the conflict, taking place within the Chief Priest himself, a conflict between personal powers, the temptation to constitute himself into an "Arrow of God" and the exigencies of public responsibility (pride and ambitions). These as treated in the novel make up the tenets of the political Igbo society and have led the Igbo to a seemingly self-destruction up till this modern times though not without other positive results.

On the first level of the crisis, the historical basis of the book "Arrow of God" is well known; it is one of the major setbacks to the British colonial administration in Nigeria. The attempts to set up warrant chiefs in the predominantly republican Igboland came to grief in the late 1920's and led to the wide spread turmoil and rioting by women, known as the Aba Women Riot (1929). This failure showed the nature of the Igbo government. The people did not look upon the warrant chiefs appointed to represent these areas as their representatives since the idea was alien to them. These warrant chiefs exploited the powers vested upon them by the British and acted rather as despots and tyrants. The people on their own part were not accustomed to such leadership, which they could not control. The Igbo, as already elaborated, usually appoint their own representative who must speak for them or be boycotted. They resented taxation because it would be used to provide salaries for the despotic Chiefs. The idea of taxation was also unfamiliar to them, fines from defaulters and occasional for a purpose being the only traditional method of raising communal funds known to them. It was ridiculous that innocent citizens should also be levied. P.C. Lloyd in Africa in Social Change published in 1972 records the failure of the experiment in indirect rule.

> In attempt to "find a Chief," men were often selected whose traditional roles had little to do with political authority. They were ritual experts or merely presided over councils of elders with equal status. Indeed, the introduction of indirect rule of the Northern Nigeria pattern to the Igbo people and their similarly organised neighbors of Eastern Nigerian proved impossible. From the beginning of the century, administrative officers had created warrant Chiefs; men who often had no traditional authority but who seemed powerful enough to act as British agents in recruiting labour. Then, when the direct taxation was introduced in 1927, widespread rioting, led by Ibo women, disclosed the extent of hostility to these warrant Chiefs. In 1930s, therefore, councils were instituted which were based upon traditional political units and their representation.

Achebe exposed the human realities in handling the historical outline that survived in that work, Arrow of God. He also treated inclusively the dilemmas facing men and women who are caught up on the historical drama, which he embodied in the person of Ezeulu.

On the second level of the crisis, continues Obiechina, lies the internal politics of Umuaro. Unlike the first level, the conflict was not as a result of culture contact. Personality deficiencies and mistaken judgment have something to do with this level. There was a kind of breakdown of the sense of solidarity among the traditionalist. Ezeulu felt this first when he perceived that his advice was set aside by the community, not once but twice in quick succession. Ezeulu reviews the situation, using the opportunity to reiterate the historical and ritual charter of his role as the first among the leaders of the clan.

> In the very distant past, when the lizards were still few and far between, the six villages - Umuachalla, Umunneora, Umuagu, Umuezeani, Umuogwugwu and Umuisiuzo lived as different people, and each worshipped its own deity. Then, the hired soldiers of Abam used to strike in the dead of night, set fire to houses and carry men, women and children into slavery. Things were so bad for the six villages that their leaders came together to save themselves. They hired a strong team of medicine men to install a common deity for them. This deity whom the fathers of the six villages made was called Ulu. Half of the medicine was buried at the place, which became the Nkwo market and the other half thrown into the stream, which became Mili Ulu. The six villages then took the name of Umuaro and the priest of Ulu became their Chief priest. From that day, an enemy never again beat them.

The authority of the Chief Priest is placed under active attack by the priest of Idemili who uses his kinsmen, the wealthy, volatile and demagogic titled elder, Nwaka of Umunneora. Idemili is one of the old gods relegated to subordinate status by the coming of Ulu. Its priest had never altogether forgotten this set back and had been in latent opposition to the priest of Ulu. From time immemorial, Ezeulu himself was aware of this fact. He knew that the priests of Idemili, Ogwugwu, Eru and Udo had never been happy with their secondary role since the villages got together and made Ulu and put him over older deities. The resentment was played down as long as the threat to collective security continued, since group solidarity is necessary to meet external threats and since only a deity, evolved in the spirit of collective solidarity, could be an adequate unifying symbol to ensure this solidarity. The colonial administration had the effect of increasing the need for collective security, since the colonial authority has taken away from the traditional authority and peoples their right to exercise judicial or even non-legal violence which became clear to the people during their land dispute with Okperi. Again, it is not surprising those institutions, which were evolved, to ensure collective security began to weaken when the threats, which gave rise to them, are no longer felt as with the case of the disappearance of Abam slave raider's threats. The super-imposition of a higher authority with a greater power of coercive violence has the effect of creating ferment in the structure of traditional authority itself. Specifically, the older gods of Umuaro accepted the dominance of Ulu as long as the old power structure remained, but now, with the imposition of a higher authority over Ulu, the minor gods see the situation as an opportunity to shake off an irksome hegemony. The resentment that lay dormant in pre-colonial days becomes active again and that was the motives of the political struggles that transpired through the novel.

In one of the most popular scene, Nwaka denied the Chief Priest of the gods in charge of collective security, the right to determine war policy. Ezeulu has just summed up their opposing attitude towards the divine in the war debate when he announced, " No matter how strong or great a man was, he should never challenge his 'Chi' to which we have seen Nwaka reply with another proverb thus; "If a man says yes, his 'Chi' also says yes". One was saying that man must be subordinate and subservient to the divine while the other insists that the divine is an expression or an agent of the human, which now raised a more fundamental problem of the nature of divinity. However, "Chi" is not really divinity as such. It is more of a personal guardian angel. Ezeulu and Nwaka believe in the same thing but Ezeulu elevated "Chi" to Chineke (God the Creator) while Nwaka continued to use "Chi" for its real meaning. This power struggle developed to the extent of Ezeulu disregarding his son's desecration of the python since it would mean submission and subordination of Eze Idemili. It also led to the instigation of the whole Umuaro by Nwaka and company to boycott their support for Ezeulu during his detention at Okperi, assuming the call by the white man to be a friendly call.

Ezeulu's spirit of revenge developed all the while he stayed in detention and even more after he had a nightmare in which Umuaro openly insults the gods. Nwaka asks, "Is there anybody here who cannot see the moon in his own compound?" Anyhow what is the power of Ulu today? Then, the people spat on the face of the Chief Priest and called him the spirit of a dead god. This led Ezeulu into taking some dangerous steps that eventually ruined the whole Umuaro and their gods. Since every man now go to become king and priest in his own compound rather than submit to any central leadership. The Christian god was there as a substitute to protect them from the religious shackles of the gods.

The third level of the crisis could be better summed up in the concept of "Ora nwe eze - The king belongs to the people" and not the people to the king, as is seen in Nwaka's demagogy. The Igbo people know no king, "Igbo Ama Eze". This is true in a sense though some Igbo communities do have kings and certainly they all recognize certain specific roles, which are defined in the social structure, and they also recognize personal achievement. The statement was used by Nwaka to disregard the role of Ezeulu. The better expression would have been "Ora Nwe Eze" because in spite of the various roles and positions recognized by the Igbo, they are worth nothing outside the support of the people. Decision and policy making is still left to the popular opinion and not to any fiat by any king. This is the traditional democracy in the strict sense. Even the powers and authority of Ezeulu could not have been without the people's support.

> Yes, it is right that the Chief Priest should go ahead and confront danger before it reached his people. That was the responsibility of the priesthood. It had been like that from the first day when the six harassed villages got together and said to Ezeulu's ancestor, you will carry this deity for us. At first, he was afraid. What power had he to carry such potent danger? But his people sang their support behind him and the flute man turned his head. So he went down on both knees and they put the deity on his head. He rose up and was transformed to a spirit. His people kept up their song behind him and he stepped forward on his first and decisive journey, compelling even the four days in the sky to give way to him.

The role of the people in the king installation is made clear here and the breakdown of such support means a breakdown of the kingship or priesthood. But Ezeulu, at this level of conflict, seems to be contemplating within himself the limits of his personal powers, the temptation to constitute himself into an arrow of God, which is in conflict with the exigencies of public responsibility. Ezeulu was not really a king in the real sense. He was a priest, some kind of a theocratic ruler

> He was merely a watchman. His power was no more than the power of a child over a goat that was said to be his. As long as the goat was alive, it was his, he would find its food and take care of it but the day it was slaughtered, he would know who the real owner was.

On the other hand, some people may argue for the existence of kingship culture among some Igbo communities especially the people of the riverine area. Professor Ejiofor, after his studies on the kingship culture in an Igbo clan, Ezechima, wrote "thus in Umuezechima, the political power resides manifestly in hierarchical institutions, but the power base is firmly with the people. It is a curious arrangement, which makes for a harmony of democracy and monarchy. It is evidence of the influence of Benin Kingship co-existing with Igbo democratic culture" (Ejiofor L 1982, p.336).

Elizabeth Isichei who also did his work on the riverine area recorded from the Ibusa community that " in early times, Ibusa had no Eze title. No one was an Ezeman. But as time went on, one Ezechi had himself crowned the Eze ofu ani Ibusa, that is, he became a single monarch like those of Ogwashi, Ubulu-Ukwu and Benin" (Isichei E 1977,p.55) " There is therefore little doubt that typical Igbo communities had no single ruler or king" (Oguejiofor J.O 1998 P.31) and that the idea of kingship is a later import. A study of the Nri theocracy may also lay proof to this fact but perhaps the Nri people may have made some ingenuous inputs that evolved the culture the way it looked, likewise was the evolution of the Aro aristocracy.

The novel "Arrow of God' for its human dimension turned into documentary that better expresses the political, social and religious nature of the Igbo man; a system that is noted for its complexity; a political system that may be summarized as segmentary and ultra democratic. A system that succeeded in rejecting hegemony as a worthy goal in politics, a system founded on the political philosophy that large is bad and small is good. The Igbo democracy has also been noted to be one of the highest development of this system of government practiced anywhere in the world. Compared with the Greek city-states, they are similar in many ways but it surpasses the Greek democracy in many ways. It gave a certain measure of government power to women, and rejecting hegemony, assured that each community or state had the right to self-government. Compared with the China city-states, it is almost superior in a sense in that amidst the inter community competitions and antagonism; it is still able to maintain the African spirit of brotherhood, both within the communities and among communities.

The democratic spirit explains the much-fragmented Igbo kingdom. Every man will divert at the slightest provocation and choose to view the moon now from his own compound, rather than be subject to any dictatorship. The absolute freedom that goes with this system allows him to do so. There is no idea of colonization of community by another, though there were community conflicts and wars but according to Uchendu," an aggressive expansionist policy does not have much meaning for the Igbo. Their expansion had been small and predatory". Expansionist wars were mostly for land grabbing not for dominance over the owners of the land. It is either for expansion of territory in which case their victim is required to leave the locality or push further and cease conflicting over a portion of land with them. Communities so afflicted have often migrated and found new clan in which they can exercise their freedom to the fullest. The inherent pride in the Igboman would lead to the break-up of some large communities where it was very difficult for a faulty leadership to make a rethink or submit easily to defeat as in the case of Ezeulu. Boycott has often become the end product of such conflicts and kingdoms continually break into smaller fragments as a result of such conflicts.

In spite of the external influence meted on the Igbo culture and the conditioning by the entity called Nigeria, the Igbo still prove to be the nation in Nigeria most disposed for democracy and democratization. The ultra democratic and anti hegemonic spirit is reiterated everywhere the Igboman is and is glaring in the new democratic setting in Nigeria today. The contentions and competitions in the chair of the Senate Presidency, the rustles in the South-Eastern-Igbo States of Anambra, Ebonyi, Enugu, Abia, and even Rivers remain the highest records of such contentions in the Third Republic of Nigeria. The clamour for an Igbo President by 2003 has continually met with the same problem; lack of unity and interest aggregation.

Due to the character of the Igbo political system, the British came to hold the view that the Igbo were the most primitive of Nigerian major ethnic nationalities. For this assumption, they found certain aspects of the Igbo culture and life baffling to explain. For instance, there were the Aro merchant network, the

Nri religious hegemony, the organised guilds of smiths at Awka, Nkwerre and Abiriba, all of whose businesses extended beyond the Igboland, then most recently, the discovery of the archeology in Igbo-Ukwu that dated to the 9th century. The Bronze pot at Bende and the pottery at Nsukka are made about 4500BC. All these raised questions about this people. Had Igbo society always been as primitive as the British thought in 1900? Had the Igbo known a golden age in the remote past and then declined? Could it be said that the Igbo once came under the influence of some alien culture carriers who by inter-breeding with them gave rise to the Nri, Awka, Nkwerre, and Abiriba and perhaps nursed the civilization at Igbo-Ukwu? Did this people rise spontaneously from Igbo society, perhaps by interacting with their environment and their neighbors?

Their answers to these questions were inspired by wrong motives and hence may not have been the appropriate answers. The answers, which the Europeans favoured, were dictated largely by the fact that they were practical administrators rather than academic investigators. Their basic interest in the matter was to find who governed the Igbo in the past in order to use such people to govern them in the century. It was easy for the Britain to rule a large area in the Northern Nigeria through the Emirs and the same was for the Western Nigeria through the established Oba's. The situation was not the same for the Igbo and the similar societies in Eastern Nigeria. Whereas, they could colonize a wide area of an Islamic state by simply signing a treaty with the Emir or defeating his army in a single war and likewise for the Yoruba and the Bini who had well established feudalism, the British in Igboland had to engage town after town and village after village for the simple reason that each of these constituted a city state with an independent government which recognized no exterior masters. As late as 1906, there were parts of Igboland, which no white man had seen and British control over the subdued areas was anything but secure and complete.

It was more or less a cardinal belief of these administrators that every society must have some kind of ruler or a chief and perhaps if there were none at present, because of crisis, that it would be a welcomed gesture to help them achieve such. This is why the British administrators thought it necessary to create structures that would resemble what they found in the north, hence found the warrant chief phenomenon. The British at the end of their studies, tended to believe that in the past, Igbo society developed under the domination of a small elite of invaders who come either from Egypt or from Yemen. They brought the idea of the "oriental hypotheses into the Igbo history and since then many writers and researchers on the Igbo history have been hoodwinked into this belief. If the British were right, why did they not proceed to rule the Igbo through the Nri and the Aro for instance? It was for this belief that the Europeans carried out many work on the Aro, Nri, Abiriba, Awka etc. the result of which was futile. The investigation produced no concrete evidence to support the theory, so it was reluctantly discarded as useless. The result is that since these researches were conducted with the bias of proving that the Aro or the Nri etc were not originally Igbo, but descendants of military conquerors from Egypt or beyond, their findings tell us little about the past of the Igbo.

Social Changes

The nature and trend of changes in the socio-political structure of the Igbo is part of the reason for which we speak of schism in Igbo culture. It also forms part of the source of controversies in the Igbo history, for instance, no Igbo man or Igbo kingdom would like to claim subordination to other kingdoms, except in few cases that are still clear in mind. They would rather speak of themselves as head. Again, it is not unnatural for a man to refute the allegation that he is a foreigner on his father's land especially when it would count on his integrity. This has been the problem with oral tradition of history. As Buah puts it, " it is easy to see that history learnt in this way can sometimes be wrong. In the first place, people tend to forget certain things as the years roll by. Also we all know that people love to exaggerate what really did take place. As the story passes on from father to son, people change it, many things are missed out...."

No one likes to point to the direction of his father's village with the left hand. As such, so many things are lost. Folklore, myths, legends and true history are at times mixed up, the ways people are governed are not told, and another thing, which often suffers in the oral tradition, is accuracy of dates. Consider where all these deficiencies are combined with the pride inherent in an Igboman, together with the much-fragmented kingdom, and see how impossible or difficult it will be to keep a historical record of the people. Several writers on Igbo history have not taken into consideration all these facts in making and putting forward the result of their research. Igbo history cannot depend absolutely on oral traditions. It has to take into cognizance and blend with other recorded events in history. It has to depend on artifacts such as archeology and to a large extent on the dialectic of thought precisely on the sociological factors of the past and present.

According to Levi Straus Claude, "Men have doubtless developed differentiated cultures as a result of geographical distance, the special feature of the environment or their ignorance of the rest of mankind, but this would be strictly and absolutely true only if every culture or society has been born and had developed without the slightest contact with any other. (Claude L.S p.99). The concept of diversity of human culture cannot be static. People continue to acquire and develop different techniques, which are sufficiently elaborate to enable them control, their environment and adopt, improve or abandon this technique as they proceed. History tells us how most of these techniques are developed. "The situation of the various cultures which have achieved the most cumulative forms of history is very similar. Such history has never been produced by isolated cultures but by cultures which voluntarily or involuntarily have combined their play and by wide variety of means (migration, borrowing, trade and warfare) have formed such coalition" (Ibid, p.126).

"Many customs come into being not because of an intrinsic need for them or of a favourable chance, but solely because of a group's desire not to be left behind by a neighboring group which is laying down specific rules in matters in which the first group had not yet thought of prescribed laws" (ibid, p.99). In other words, cultures could be borrowed or changed from within. In Africa for instance, "the subject of African culture and agent of change pre-supposes the principles of dynamics and mechanics of culture. The study must note the substitutive process in which a new cultural element replaces an existing one, and fits into a culture so perfectly that the new element functions with minimal or no structural institutional change...this substitutive process may also work simultaneously with the additive process in which new elements do not replace existing one but add to them without also introducing crisis or conflict of values. The additive process can also operate in two directions. First, when a culture is able to receive new good cultural elements from another showing itself as a resilient culture and secondly, when it can induce and produce changes within its own native gains showing itself alive and dynamic" (Onwubiko 1986 P.)

The Igbo culture is marked by its readiness to accept changes. Partly, the socio-political structure and the worldview formed the bases for their receptivity to change. The Igbo show a sense of pragmatism. There are really very few absolutes in Igbo traditions. "The Igbo sometimes possess unbelievable ability to endure hardship. This hardship must, in some manner, be perceived as the best option under the given circumstances. This means that if a better alternative is seen, they will readily abandon their former option for the latter one" (Oguejiofor P.25). They hardly believe in any kind of determinism. For instance, in "Things Fall Apart" despite the destiny of Unoka, Okonkwo's father, Okonkwo believed that he could change his future by hard work.

One important aspect of the change in Igbo tradition is that, apart from the changes in the culture that are determined by historical, geographical and sociological circumstances, the Igbo are more readily receptive to changes that they have reasons to make. The example of such reasoned dynamism are found in Things Fall Apart, when Ogbuefi Ezeudu, who was the oldest man in the town was telling two other men who came to visit him how the punishment for breaking the week of peace of "Ani" had become very mild.

> My father told me that he had been told that in the past, a man who broke the peace was dragged on the ground through the village until he died. But after a while, this custom was stopped because it spoilt the peace, which it was meant to preserve.

We are also able to notice from this discussion that this sort of change is an internally induced one, that is, when the people reasoned for themselves and realized the custom to be bad.

> Somebody told me yesterday, said one of the younger men, that in some clan it is an abomination for a man to die during the week of peace. It is indeed true said Ogbuefi Ezeudu. They have that custom

in Obodoani if a man dies at this time he is not buried but cast into the evil forest. It is a bad culture, which these people observe; they lack understanding. They throw away large number of men and women without burial and what is the result? Their clan is full of evil spirit of these unburied dead, hungry to do harm to the living".

Okonkwo's friend Obierika, on another hand, observed the discomfort caused by the law that forbade titled man to climb palm tree, which to him is filled with contradictions.

I don't know how we got that law, said Obierika. In many other clans, a man of title is not forbidden to climb the palm tree. Here, we say he cannot climb the tall tree but he can tap the short one standing on the ground. It is like Dimaragana, who will not lend his knife for cutting up dog's meat because the dog was taboo to him, but offered to use his teeth

For the Igboman, the past is indeed very important but should not constitute a crippling absolute. This attitude has had a tremendous impact on the people, their culture and religion. Things did not stagnate despite the confrontation that marked the contact with the Europeans, which led to some of them describing the Igbo by some early European anthropologists as "the most lawless part of Nigeria" (C.K Meek 1937 P.2). The situation was different with the missionaries. The missionaries came, with time, to acquire a good reputation among the Igbo when the people actually felt that they had some good will for them. Though this was through a combination of factors including the giving of charity and the evident stance of some of the missionaries against the brutalities perpetrated against the people by the British Trading Companies. The missionaries were received peacefully. But their work did not initially attract many people except that some people sent in their slaves and the least privileged children, together with the outcasts (osu). These formed the foundation of the Christian villages.

"However, it was not until the missionaries started the work of education, something that certainly promised a better future for the Igbo that they witnessed an almost unbelievable explosion of converts to their message. In many instances, Igbo communities went out of their way to invite missionaries, first to establish mission stations, and then to run schools among them. Often, in addition to providing land, they also had to build the school and pay the teachers from their meager income. To do so, they levied themselves and provided labour" (Oguejiofor P.26). The case of Ojiako Ezenne, the warrant chief of Adazi Nnukwu is a life example of this history. He is renowned for building one of the earliest schools in Igboland and inviting the white missionaries, Frs. Lidan and Bubendorf, housing them and feeding them for a period of 30 years with the motive of educating his people through these missionaries. This formed the basic missionary tool used by the missionaries in converting the Igbo. Many of the people themselves did not go to school. They sent their children to school with all the support they needed. A good example of this reaction is seen in Ezeulu in "Arrow of God" who in spite of being the ritual leader of tradition in Umuaro had an eye of fancy for the white man's education. He sent in his son Oduche despite all odds reasoning to his friend in defense that " to see well enough of a new masquerade, one does not need to watch it from one angle'. In other words, he was sending Oduche as an eye on the white man. What was the result? These children sent to school in turn accepted to be Christians and thus began the story of one of the most phenomenal successes of missionary endeavour in the history of Christianity in its entirety. Ezeulu for instance, was shocked that his own son should be one of the greatest fanatics as to lock a sacred python in a box. The historical evidence of the truth still lies in almost every community where all the earlier built churches are seen to lie side by side with a school of the old structure type. This is the route through which the Igbo came to Christianity.

The question relevant at this particular time in the development of Igbo history and changes is, to what extent has these changes been retained? Of course, the Igbo materialism and inclination for acquisition has inspired all these changes. Recently, people were searching on the current decline on education, especially among Igbo male children. Perhaps, the reason cannot be any other but the decline in benefits from education, reasonably because of the economic decline in the country since after the 70's and perhaps for the trend that developed after the civil war, which rendered the Igbo, and their southern brothers without equal employment opportunities as their fellow Nigerians. Professional courses became the main relevant education pursued by Igbo male kids or at best they opt for self-reliance in a business where he is able to control his resources.

The situation in religion also calls for a state of emergency. The missionaries would have counted their successes in gathering a sizable flock into the church, through the school. Of course, the white man knew that by mere getting hold of all the children who are the future generation, they have practically taken hold of the entire race. The proliferation of religion and sprouting of churches here and there calls for a novel study of this people, a historical study, which will perhaps produce a better understanding and relations with the Igbo.

About the changes that occurred in the historical anthropology of the Igbo people, it is good to remark with Leiris Michel that culture " being identified with a way of life peculiar to a specified human society in a specified epoch, a culture, however slow its evolution can never be entirely static insofar at least as it exist as an organised system, recognizable despite its variations, it is the appanage of a group which is constantly changing through the mere process of death and birth. Its radius (i.e. membership) may increase or decrease, but at every point in its history, it consist exclusively of elements socially transmissible (by inheritance or borrowing) and hence, though there are bound to be modifications or even major alterations, with the rejection of former elements and the addition of new, the culture itself is able to continue through all the transformations of the fluid group it represents and share its hazards or disasters, assimilate new elements and export certain of its own, more or less replace the culture of a different group (through conquest or otherwise) or conversely be absorbed by another culture (Leaving few or no visible trace behind it). Clearly then, a culture is essentially a provisional and infinitely flexible system."

It would be a false notion then to believe that the Igbo have no sense of history because of the receptivity to change. It would rather fit to say that the Igbo are ever ready to change for an end in view and would never like to be left behind in social movements. His readiness to do certain things is nevertheless owed to some underlying traits, which can be channeled to laudable and sometimes despicable goals. Basden also remarked about the Igbo immigrants "whatever the conditions, the Ibo immigrants adapted themselves to meet them, and it is not long before they make their presence felt in the localities where they settle". (Basden T.K. 1966 p.11.

Besides, we may also bring into the judgment the population pressure that is intense among the Igbo people and generally in South-Eastern Nigeria, which forced the Igbo to embrace migration in spite of its precariousness.

Chapter 2

The Critique of Postulations on Igbo Origin

There are the various folklores, myths, genealogies, histories etc that had been proposed by people as being the story of the Igbo origin. I want therefore to take a critical look at the works propounded by scholars with a view to settling their discrepancies.

It is evident that many scholars on Igbo history have disagreed on this topic, each finding the other's work wanting, while some will even be dismissed out right by some as sublime nonsense. The different accounts of Igbo traditions of origin have been classified into two. The classes are referred to as "the cultural traditions of migration and the cultural traditions of non-migration" (Onwubiko O, 1991).

Traditions of Non-Migration

Accounts that fall under this heading seem to require a serious critical review. Judging from an anthropological point of view, these accounts seem to have failed to see the relationship between all races both within themselves and among other races. From a religious point of view, different religions have their own various but unified account of creation of mankind. On the social level, different races or ethnic groups have theirs. Would it not be ridiculous and superfluous if a scientific work such as the one we have at hand would have to accept every account of creation including accounts that do not stretch beyond the 16th century? How do we blend the religious, anthropological and social points of view on origin of man? If they cannot be blended, which view do we hold in esteem? As regards the African circumstance, through which of the viewpoints can we really understand and find the true origin of a race like the Igbo in a new world order? Perhaps, it is through a view that is most scientific without neglecting the contributions from other views.

In modern study made by people that hold the view of non-migration, we read "some scholars mapped out a 'nuclear area' in Igboland where people believed they were created in their present homes". (Onwubiko, O. 1991 p.8). Uchendu in his work, Igbo of Southeast Nigeria, observed that " this belt formed by Owerri, Awka, Orlu and Okigwe division constitute this nuclear area. Its people have no belief of coming or migrating from any other place. We assume an early migration from this area into Nsukka-Udi highlands in the North and the Ikwere, Etche, Asa and Ndoki in the South. The Eastern Isuama claim to have come from this center. Ngwa traditions point to their secondary migration from Mbaise"….(Uchendu, V.C; 1965 P.3).

A clear reflection on the first statement of Uchendu which ascertained Owerri, Awka, Orlu and Okigwe as the division that constitute the nuclear areas where people believed that they were created will bring us to thinking about areas far apart. We shall then end up in proving four (4) different accounts of creation of the Igbo race, yet that may not be all. This statement may have been articulated from considering the differences in dialects and the little disparity in cultures among these areas. But how could they have come to a crescendo and unite to form one culture and refer to themselves as Igbo? We may assume the disparity found among the people dwelling on the borderlines at Nsukka, Etche, Asa, Ndoki, Ikwere, Abakaliki, Ibusa etc. from the main land, from the point of view of external influence from other cultures but not accepting just the same for the main lands or giving as many accounts as there are many different dialects in language and disparity in culture.

Such accounts may not fall within the domains of science based on the recent discoveries and disclosures on human anthropology, genealogy and geology. It is ridiculous to consider the views that men were created in different parts of the world and, worse still, at different times, some of which dating after the 16th century A.D. Natural anthropology gives us different accounts of the origin of man from such animal species like the Homo Sapiens and the Homo Erectus via Homo Faber, Homo habilis etc.

Two main theories have been proposed to explain the origin of all living beings

1. The theory of fixism holds that various species were directly created or made by God, as we know them today.

2. The theory of evolution claims that the various forms of life which we know today originated gradually by natural descent, from one or a few original living beings (Donceel J.F, 1967; P.7)

The first theory, according to Donceel, is only theoretically tenable. God could have made each individual species either simultaneously when life began on earth or each one at its appointed time.

However, he did not consider that the same specie or race could have many different account of creation, as there are nations or tribes in them. Evolution on the other hand has been admitted to occur by all scientists from evidence from comparative anatomy, paleontology, embryology, biogeography and genetics. Charles Darwin (1807-1882), Hugo De Vries (1848-1925) and Lamarch (1744-1829) were the promulgators of this theory.

"Biologists now agree that all men everywhere belong to a single species, Homo sapiens. As is the case with other species, all men share their essential hereditary characters in common, having received them from common ancestors. Other hereditary characters vary from person to person and where marriages occur chiefly within local populations, isolated from other populations by geographical and similar barriers, some of these characters tend to become more concentrated in some groups than in other more distant ones. If these separations are long continued in terms of hundreds or thousands of generations, such populations tend to differ from each other in the relative commonness or rarity of hereditary characteristics. Races arising in this way are thus seen to differ rather in degree than in kind" (L.C. Dunn, Race & Biology, pg. 31).

History on its own part has continued from where research of biologists and the speculations of the evolutionists began and have recorded different accounts of developments and migrations of races and people. In spite of the fact that Africa (south of the Sahara) has not been known for a long time, sciences (Evolution) has succeeded in providing the evidences from paleontology (fossils) that the black race and probably all the races have their origin in Africa judging from the dating of the fossils remains from the Oligocene period (parapithecus). The disparity in colour and physical outlook of various races can simply be attributed to have developed on the climatic condition of the region occupied by each or perhaps on miscegenation.

From this level of scientific understanding, how could such riddles be resolved if we are to go by the words of people like the elder from Nguru Mbaise, Onuoha Dunu? He said to Mr. L.O Nwaliri as recorded by Isichei, "we did not come from anywhere and anyone who tells you we came from anywhere is a liar, write it down" (Isichei E, 1976;P.3). Perhaps, we could find some fossils here; anthropologists have not affirmed this since nothing has happened to stimulate the vigilance of anthropologist towards this area. The statement may simply be described as having an undertone of pride. From the Igbo ideology, "is there any man who cannot see the moon from his own compound?" comes the idea, "is there any man who cannot write the history on his own?". Here lies the crux of the problem in writing the history of this race. This is part of the mentality that has left a great part of the Igbo history lost, except for the most recent migrations.

However, in as much as we argue this, we still have to treasure in the mind that the Negroid specie to which the Igbo belong evolved here in Africa and may have separated and scattered over the continent very early. Yet, to accept such history of non-migration as we are presented with will be baseless since there are no such artifacts as fossils or ancient deposits that would form a footstool for such speculations. The known facts are so little and short and do not stretch so far into the past. They only come to an end where the trend of descent grows thin and comes to a break (cannot go any further). The disgusting side of this is that scholars who attempt to trace the lineage ridiculously posit this point of breakage as the origin.

Michel Leiris on his defense against racism and culture wrote, "While undoubtedly there are idiosyncrasies in addition to those distinguishing individuals, which may be broadly regarded as differentiating the members of a particular society from the rest of the world, it is under the head of acquired behaviour that they will be found. They are thus by definition cultural". (Leiris M. P.152).

As I have already pointed out, no man would accept allegation on his being a foreigner in his land. It is quite a natural process that he would refute such allegation. To defend this, he has to promulgate a culture of non-migration however incoherent it might seem. The natural traits will have to be studied and understood in dealing with the kind of history like that of the Igbo race.

Traditions Of Migrations

There are many traditions of migration found in Igbo culture. These migrations range from migrations of small parts or lineages of bigger communities to movement of whole community. The reason for such migrations may be population pressure, lack of support from the land, expulsion by bigger communities through defeat in wars or traditional beliefs in necessitated movement by theological understanding. The movement or migration may be a temporary or permanent relocation to a nearby area or over a wide distance across rivers and forests. In all the migrations, the same culture was carried on and maintained all through where some in addition develop a great sense of solidarity and are able to pledge to home community, cultural subordination and sell out of their culture to new lands where they migrate to. I may just have to concentrate on the big migrations, which perhaps will give a fair detail of migrations in the past.

The Aro Culture

The result of the lack of a central organ for effective governance among the Igbo is the hegemony of the Aro on Igboland. The Aro people are more or less an Igbo group, which incorporated Ibibio elements. They came from Arochukwu in the Eastern border of Igboland. The town is near the Cross River and is in strategically geographic position with regard to the Igbo to the North and West and to the Efik and Ibibio to the East and South with their slave centers at the mouth of the Calabar and Cross River to the South. The people were fierce and adventurous priests and merchants who saw in the limited nature of the Igbo tribal organization opportunities for the expansion of trade and influence. They dominated the Igbo and the Ibibio through their various settlements, their famous oracle, the long Juju- "Ibini Ukpabi". It is good to note here that the term Arochukwu is a colonial nomenclature. The primitive term for this people is Aro-Oke-Igbo or simply Oke-Igbo.

Today, the Aro may claim to be the real heirs of Igboland and the aborigine of the tribe. They may also claim to possess the birthright of the first son among the Igbo, and claim their culture to be the unique and central Igbo culture. Unless such claims are viewed axiomatically, the truth may not become visible.

> The Aro live on the West bank of the Cross River near the Itu. Tradition says that the Aro village group included people of non-Ibo descent. Aro tradition tells us that an Ibo settler rose up in revolt against his Ibibio landlord. The settler consulted an Ibo doctor friend who arranged to invite some raiders of the Akpa (a tribe on the East bank of the Cross River) to fight the Ibibio residents. They were successful, but as one of the Akpa warriors was killed, the Ibo settler was held responsible and he had to flee. However, the doctor made peace between the Akpa and the Ibo and after swearing a covenant, they lived happily ever after. These were the three main subjects that made up the present Aro. (Stride G.T & Ifeka C; 1977, P.7)

They altogether, make up a total of nineteen villages seven of which claim descent from the Igbo doctor's son, six villages claim to be descended from the Akpa warriors and five derive from the Igbo settler. There were also some Ibibio element in the village group which probably made up the last village though retaining only very little of their Ibibio characteristics. The senior living descent of the Igbo doctor holds the title of Eze-Aro or Chief of Aro.

The political power of the Aro like the other Igbo is built around the oracle and its effectiveness in the village group is in the hands of the elders who try to keep the secrets of the oracle from public knowledge. Through such way, the oracle helped the Aro to develop a more central sense of politics, solidarity and unity than existed elsewhere in Igboland. It was this mentality that they went ahead to export to the hinterland of the Igbo by marketing the popularity of the oracle.

The oracle at Arochukwu became so famous in the whole of Igboland for several reasons. "Ibini Ukpabi" as the oracle is called has the most efficient and prosperous network of agents' known in Igboland. The Aro middlemen monopolized the slave trade and deal on other commodities.

Secondly, people are charmed by the ability of this oracle to administer immediate justice, which other oracles do not do or do only at rare occasions or at slow pace. Though it has been lately disclosed that such ability to administer immediate justice especially by killing litigants who invoked the oracle falsely is not just only supernatural but also somehow politically man-made. A different secret form of network agent also operates. This takes hold of such litigants along the bushy and dwindling path to the oracle and they were never seen again. People saw trails of blood flowing out of the oracle and this was taken to prove that the guilty was dead (by mysterious means).

> However, old informants told early British district officers that the Ibini Ukpabi Oracle Priest of Arochukwu used to sacrifice animals whose blood was then seen flowing out from the grove. The litigant was hidden for a few days and later sold into slavery. It was in such manner that justice was done. (Stride G.T 7 Ifeka C; 1977 P.350.

The secret power of the oracle lies on the fact that all protect the mysteries behind it collectively. The agents that direct people to the oracle have an onus to bring a report or information about the litigant before they get to the oracle. He also has the onus to investigate the case and bring the report about the case before hand. The litigant on arrival, have their names called by the oracle chief who already has every data about them. He tells them everything about them and their case without their speaking about it claiming that he got the information through the oracle's divination. With such mesmerism, the litigants now bow to and are ready to accept everything from the oracle as divine and true. These acts of the Aro are taken from the importance of mystery as a principle for the sustenance of every religion.

The oracle chief considers the information as received from the litigants and the agents and dispenses justice on behalf of the oracle by poisoning the convict during oat taking or by allowing him to disappear in the dwindling bushy path by the operation of the agents. Significantly, on the other hand, the other party is allowed to go home and tell the story.

For the ignorance of the people on the operation of the oracle and his priest, it is likely that on the whole, litigants being convinced of the famous oracle's power and fearing the wrath of it, would tell the truth.

The third reason for Ibini Ukpabi's fame is that the commercial and vital activities of the Aro have a mutual reinforcing effect. They make a lot of money and valuables from the oracle by telling people to bring this or that for sacrifices, selling captured litigants into slavery, fees and taxes for providing passage (escort) to the deity etc. These give them some economic power that most of them do not have to farm, so they all take the collective responsibility of spreading the name and fame of the oracle to an increasing number of clients.

However, there are some other oracles in Igboland that came close to the same level as the "Ibini Ukpabi" and so became also widely renowned mainly for their impartial verdict. The "Agballa" oracle of Awka, the "Igweke Ala" oracle of Umunoha and the "Amadioha" oracle of Ozuzu, whereas there are other oracles that gained little or no recognition like "Udo", "Ogwugwu" and "Idemili".

It is very important to note here that most of these oracles in the main land of the Igbo like Udo's, Ogwugwu's and Idemili's are disregarded because the mechanism of their operations are almost common knowledge, so people had little or no confidence in them. They rather resort to the oracles they know little of and from which they get some sort of mesmerization. These are the further away oracles, which they believe should be more effective whereas the ineffectiveness of their oracle lie in their being known soldiers. Such beliefs and practices promoted these "foreign" oracles at the expense of indigenous oracles.

The Aro established various settlements throughout Igboland. Through these, they dominated the local markets. They specialised in the buying and selling of slaves and from then, the coastal states received their export trades. The Aro trade route radiated to all directions and through these they dominated the local population. Their domination depended largely on their influence as oracle agents and leaders. The influence therefore could not be said to amount to any comprehensive political control. The clan of Afikpo, Okigwe, Uturu, Aba, Owerri, Onitsha, Nsukka, Ohuhu, Ngwa, for example, were only dominated but not conquered or taxed as such whereas, some towns did not feel the Aro hegemony. The Aro also played different clans one against another, to obtain plenty of slaves. Some of these places have Aro settlement, trading centers and shopping places connected by protected trade route.

Aro is believed, deployed mercenary soldiers in Igbo inter-village wars in order to facilitate the capture of the slaves for exports. These kept the trade routes safe and passed gangs of collected slaves to the exchange centers. They usually devastated those clans, which were considered recalcitrant or hostile to the Aro. A better understanding of the state of affairs during this period of threat is a reference to the Umuaro village episode in "Arrow of God". When the six villages had to come together to save themselves (collective security) against the Abam and Aninta warriors.

> In the very distant past, when lizards were still few and far between, the six villages; Umuachalla, Umunneora, Umuagu, Umuezeani, Umuogwugwu and Umuisiuzo lived as different people and each worshipped its own deity. The hired soldiers of Abam used to strike in the dead of the night, set fire to houses and carry men, women and children into slavery. Things were so bad for the six villages that their leaders came together to save themselves. (Achebe C;"Arrow of God" P.14).

One now can see clearly the historical setting of Achebe's work and can as well imagine the period of such historical events.

Again, one may review the situation at this time with the work of the African (French) slave Olaudah Equiano in his book, 'Equiano's travel'. Equiano is probably the first Igbo writer, and wrote his autobiography about 1789. The book was written in French and later translated into English as "The interesting Narrative of the life of Olaudah Equiano or Gustavus Vassa the African" or simply called "Equiano's Travel".

As indicated in the narrative, Olaudah was born about 1745 to an Igbo clan. He narrated the beautiful life in Igboland before he was kidnapped together with his sister and sold into slavery. Passing from one hand to the other, he finally came to the hands of his eventual master, a Frenchman who was a sea captain, he re-baptized him Gustavus Vassa and he remained in his hands until he was able to buy his freedom. He was quite intelligent, energetic, hardy etc. just like a typical Igbo man. His exposition as a ship captain's slave benefited him so much. He gave himself reasonable education and proceeded to write his book in which he attempted to give the rest of the world the true image of Africa and the ugly face of slavery.

"He aimed to show that Africa had an indigenous system of government, and ways of maintaining law and order; that Africa had an indigenous culture to be proud of; a culture of happy people, of a nation of dancers, musicians and poets. He showed that there was some form of education in Africa in which the children were educated within the culture to be morally truthful; that there was the idea of God (Supreme Being) already in existence in Africa before its contact with Christianity. That African (Igbo) has very rich culture likened to that of the Jews and finally, Equiano wanted to expose the extent of damage done to African culture by slave trade. Here, he narrated the feeling of leaving ones home and family and flashed the exploit of the slave raiders (Aro) in his life".

(Equiano O; Equiano's travel, P. Edwards (Ed) London, Heinemann, 1967.

"My father, besides many slaves had numerous family of which seven lived to grow up including myself and a sister…one day, when all our people were gone to their works as usual and only I and my dear sister were left to mind the house, two men and a woman got over our walls and in a moment seized us both and without giving us time to cry or make resistance, they stopped our mouths and ran off with us into the nearest wood".

The Aro were very wealthy and as a result were able to keep large teams of mercenaries. If two clans were in conflict, the Aro could obtain mercenaries for one for a few against the other. They scouted the clan or village to be attacked and would pass on information to the mercenaries who would use it for a surprise attack. The heads of those killed are kept for ceremonial and prestigious displays (see the Umuofia warriors of "Things Fall Apart"). Okonkwo had six skulls that he holds as evidence for having killed six men at war.

The captives will be sold as slaves. It is assumed that Ohofia and Abiriba people mostly served as these mercenaries. All these were happening just some few years before the arrival of the European in the 19th Century.

The Aro oracle filled the vacuum left by lack of central organs of settling disputes in the tribal organizations. Their position as an absolute arbiter of the oracle was a fundamental factor in the hegemony of the Aro. The Aro believed that the oracle was with them wherever they went. This offered them the best psychological build-up that they needed. It had informants and the people organised their information service system so well that the oracle's fairness and knowledge of facts were recognized throughout the Igboland. Inter-clan dispute were referred to the oracle at the inducement of the agents. All those who were found guilty were likely to be "chopped" by the oracles. It could not only give verdict on a dispute but could also enforce its decision on the offenders. In this way, the Aro used the oracle to dominate Igboland who lacked any force to unite the different clans by peace or war against the Aro warlords.

There were however, other oracles as I have earlier mentioned, these included the "Agballa", "Igwekala" etc but quite unlike the oracle of Arochukwu, and these lacked extensive settlements and the networks of the Aro type. They were nevertheless influential in trade, judicial and religious matters over considerable areas. They depended on religious atmosphere alone for the enforcement of their verdicts and their influence began to wane when the disease or curse failed to descend on the disobedient and finally, during the dominance of the Christian religion and the European conquest and rule. A practical reference can also be made to the Ulu of "Arrow of God". The older gods of Umuaro and the people accepted Ulu's power as long as the old power structure remained. However, when the imposition of a higher authority over Ulu came in (British rule), the powers of Ulu began to wane. The minor gods saw the situation as an opportunity to shake off an irksome hegemony. Just in a similar way, all the gods in Igboland lost their reputation to the new religion.

Like the Ulu, which was responsible for collective security, it was the military and the religious aspect of the Aro oracle that have combined to give it ascendancy over the other oracles. It definitely became a national cult. The mercenary soldiers enforced its decisions. It imposed fines, which were paid in terms of slaves, and the soldiers intervened where the payment was delayed or neglected. Thus, the Aro used oracle troops to compel the Igbo to recognize their leadership and accept their suggestions and advice. The oracle was the force behind their operations in Igboland. They continued to dominate because there was no central authority either indigenous or foreign to bring all the part of Igboland under complete control. The effects of such events in the past are still visible in Igbo communities. As recorded by Achebe, the six villages of Umuaro, which had to come together to save themselves, is a record of the events that took place in Igboland. So many communities today in Igboland are formed by so many different elements, all-coming from different places and at different times, which is a result of such events of history. Communities are pushed out of their settlement if they cannot wage war against bigger clans. The result is a move by smaller clans to merge together to form a greater force. These moves however, created longer lasting problems as we see today, since many communities today are yet to achieve peace within. Rarely do we find any Igbo community today that is not heterogeneous. It is also part of the reason why most of the Igbo history is lost today.

The Aro established settlements in Igboland and are still found in such places as Ajalli, Ndikelionwu, Amaokpala, Ndiokpalaeze, Arondizuogu, Arochukwu village of Ihiala etc. A living witness to the Aro's history of accumulating war mercenaries in the past is the Arondizuogu Community of Okigwe Local Government Area. This is very evident in the names to start with. A part of the community is known as the Aro, which are principally made up of Aro elements, who originated from Aroamankwu in Arochukwu where they still have their homes while the other part is known as Ndizuogu, literary meaning war allies or war mercenaries. The villages and the characteristics of this section show very much that they are a collection of various elements a good number of which originates from Aguata, Agbaenu, Amaiyi, Aniocha, Orlu, Ideato, Nnewi and Orumba areas. Some were captured in wars and raids while some willingly joined the Aro caravan for one reason or the other ranging from economic to social ostracizing. This explains why there are lots of cultural similarity among these areas both in language and culture. The culture in Ndizuogu also imbibes various other Igbo characteristics, which explains why they seem to have climaxed above other Igbo cultural areas in culture projection. Most of the people of this community still remember and can trace their origin. As many come to Igbo-Ukwu, Ezinifite, Isuofia, Amaiyi etc and various parts of Aguata and Igboland to commune with their blood brothers. Likewise, are the elements of other Aro settlements that still go back to Arochukwu during great feasts like the Ikeji festival? Today, the Aro still claim the right to break kola-nut, which in Igboland is a symbol of superiority. They are still proud of their golden past but are their golden past any shore on which to build the history of the whole Igbo? Matthew's work at Arochukwu during the colonial era did not even yield any results on which to build such conclusion. The idea of Igbo Land coming under Egyptian influence and that the spread of the Egyptian culture in Igbo Land was the work of a small elite group who after inter breeding with the people became the Nri and Aro of today is only an illusion what I call the "oriental illusion" in this work. The hair splitting efforts to create linkages with the Hamite and the fanciful tale of how their ancestors were part of Jewish community who were expelled from Spain by Ferdinand and Isabella all fell to the lots of this illusion. My reasons will become clearer as this work proceeds.

The Nri Culture

It is thought that Eri was the apical ancestors and eponymous founder of Umu-Nri. As first recorded by M.D.W. Jeffreys;

> According to Umueri mythology, their ancestor Eri came down from heaven and sat on an anthill because the earth was a morass or waterlogged. To use the Igbo phrase "ala di deke deke". When Eri complained, Chukwu sent a blacksmith with his bellows, fire and charcoal to dry up the land. When the blacksmith finished his work, Eri rewarded him with 'ofo', which conferred on him special claims to the smiting profession and had him settled at Awka. (Onwubiko, O. 1991; P.9)

This even though called a mythology, as mentioned by Onwubiko, like the Greek and other mythologies had in itself some fundamental reality. It is simply graded on the level of mythology because it fell among those sort of history that tend to fabricate an origin or a start at the point where it can no longer go further on the trend of descent. As we shall later find in this book, such history has really some connection with the real. This however, should not be left as verbose as it now stands supposing that God created the Nri where they now exist, just to escape the claim of being immigrants on their present lands.

However, it is good to note that, "when we are concerned with cultures which have left behind no written records or buildings, and which employed very primitive techniques (as is true for one half of the inhabited world and for 90-99 percent, varying according to region, of the time since the dawn of civilization) it may be said that we can really know nothing of them, and that our best effort at understanding them can be no more than suppositions". (Claude Strauss; P.104).

The colonial administrators who found the Igbo societal structure so difficult and so took on the task to find the best possible channel to rule this people basically stimulated the postulations on Eri culture. Ethnographers and anthropologists like A.G Leonard's, P.A.Talbot, NorthcoteW.Thomas, G.T.Basden, M.D.W.Jeffreys were the first to publish works on the Eri culture. Their work basically only affirmed some religious and ritual activities of the Eri. These works were followed by the work of M.A.Onwuejeogwu in which he splitted his hairs in trying to link the Igbo-Ukwu culture with the Eri. Other notable writers on the Eri include I.C.K.Idigo, C.M.Ezekwugo and Emmanuel Ifesieh. The works of these authors and others on Eri show that they did not heed the solemn warning of Claude Strauss in linking this culture to the Igbo-Ukwu culture and proclaiming it as the Igbo culture

According to professor Ifesieh, Eri took the title of Nri with the sacred symbol of 'Ofo' and 'Alo'. However, there has been a controversy on:

1. *Who took the title of Nri, Eri or his son? And*

2. *Whether 'Nri' was a title, a common or a proper name?*

3. *Also, there is a question mark on who was the first son of Eri.*

To the first question, there are two versions belonging to the same tradition.

The authors of the first version include Jeffreys and Henderson who did their fieldwork on Agukwu around 1930 and reiterated by Onwuejeogwu. According to their works, it was not Eri but Agukwu who took the title Nri and has claimed it as both a title and a proper name (Agukwu-Nri and Nri). They also maintained that Agukwu-Nri was the first son of Eri and that it was his son and daughter that "Chukwu" ordered to be killed in order to secure food for the rest of the Igbo people.

The authors of the second version headed by Anadi holds that it was Eri who took the title, Nri, which means "Supreme King". He asserted that Eri took this title with two religious symbols 'Ofo' and 'Alo'. Nri to him is not a proper name or a common name but a religious title to any validly consecrated and ruling divine king of children of Eri. It was this version also which holds that Agukwu-Nri is not the first son of Eri. It has it that Eri got the following six children: -

1. *Agulu Nnamenyi who was the father of Agulu-Eri*

2. *Meniru who begot the ancestors that begot:*

   a) *Okpala Kanu, Okpala-Nnamu and Aguinyi, who was the father of Enugwu-Ukwu (Umueri, a part of Neni town) Nawfia, Enugwu-Agidi, all of the same mother.*

   b) *Ifiukwuanam begot Agukwu*

c)   *Namoko begot Ozu, Diodo (section of Akamkpisi) Ovolo (Mbaukwu) and Avo.*

d)   *Avo begot Ora-Eri and Nnokwa.*

e)   *The mother of Ekwenanuka clans of Akamkpisi was Meniru's daughter.*

3.   *Onogu Begot Igbariam*

4.   *Olin Odudu begot Amanuke*

5.   *Iguedo was tattooed daughter and the mother of Umuleri, Nando, Awkuzu and Ogbunike.*

6.   *Onoja, his mother was Oboli. Tradition has it that he (Onoja) founded the Nri kingdom of Idah. (Anadi, 1972, P14)*

Michael Onwuejeogwu in his famous writing 'Odinani', exposed the various connotations of Nri, which made the word very much ambiguous. He designated the name Nri to have five connotations: -

> 1. The name of a territory occupied by the king of Nri (Nri) and his people, who according to oral tradition migrated from around Aguleri the North on the River Anambra. At Aguleri, Eri the father of Nri established a sacred kingship in antiquity. Nri left Aguleri and migrated South wards into Igboland and established the Nri theocratic hegemony in the present Nri town. According to Nri traditions, a branch hived off to Ora-eri to establish another Nri theocracy. Ora-Eri is situated immediately to the North of Igbo-Ukwu. Nri lay 18km (10miles) further north, not far from Awka, made up of three major villages of Diodo, Akamkpisi and Agukwu, by which latter name it is marked on some maps.

> 2. The name of a people directly under the Eze Nri. In the past, Nri men performed politics-ritual services in Ibo settlements. They were known by the Ichi scarification marks on their faces. They moved from village to village carrying in their hands the staff of political and ritual authority. They were regarded as sacrosanct and might not be

killed or molested. They were both the symbol and agents of inter-village peace and friendliness. By the authority vested on them by the Eze Nri, they were believed to possess powers of cleansing the abominations of the earth, making and dissolving the Igbo code of avoidance and taboo, explaining and enacting any new regulations of ritual and political behaviour, arbitrating and making peace between villages, ordaining title holders and repairing pollutions against community.

3. The name of a culture. This culture seems to have been born and nurtured in the upper valley of the River Anambra at some fairly remote period and then later diffused southwards and westwards. Michael Onwuejeogwu believes that it was Nri culture, which developed the concept of Chi-Ukwu (Great God) theocratic monarch who controlled the earth force by the use of ceremonial staff. He also believes that Nri politico-ritual hegemony declined between AD 1400 and AD 1700. In 1911, the British Colonial Administration liquidated it, but something of the ritual influence continued.

4. The name of the people who claim to have some kind of connection with Nri. In the past, many towns for prestige and political reasons associated themselves with Nri calling themselves the children of Nri. Such settlements occur both between the Western and Eastern Ibo. They also claim a distant relationship with certain clans in Igala to the Northwest of Igboland, through the legendary Onojaobomi, who according to Nri genealogy, was the second son of Eri and migrated to Igala country.

5. The name given to the highest politico-ritual title. In all Igbo settlements, West and East of the River Niger, there are various graded titles culminating in the taking of 'Eze', 'Ozo', 'Obi' or 'Nze' title. The highest title in places that adopted monarchy such as Onitsha is 'Obi', while the places that did not, the highest title is 'Nze', 'Ozo' or 'Eze'. However, in Nri and Ora-Eri, the Eze takes the title Nri and thus Eze Nri. Nri is the highest politico-ritual title found in settlements at the Nri culture areas. (Onwuejeogwu M.A; Odinani vol. 1 No.1 1972).

Though there seem to be a persistent controversy about the use of the word Nri as a group of people as such by Onwuejeogwu, the term Nri has come to denote a sub-tribe or clan, which comprises Aguleri, Umuleri, Nteje, Igbariam, Amanuke, Urunebo, Enugwu-Ukwu and Ora-Eri. The word Nri should therefore be used to mean "a group of people", "a tribe", town among Umueri and not Umunri town. Agukwu is posing at the expense of his cousin, that he is the only Nri town. The correct historical terminology as held by some should be Umueri because he was the first divine king and their father.

However, there have been a lot of controversies over supremacy among the clans. Some people from Agukwu even affirm Onwuejeogwu's work that some towns without any Nri lineage associate themselves with the word so as to gain some social recognition.

> The people of Nri (Agukwu) contend that they are the first immigrants into this part of Igboland and being the aboriginal inhabitants they have to break kola in any gathering of people of the area. This relation between Agukwu-Nri and Aguleri has been clearly studied and there is sufficient evidence to conclude that Menri's the founder of Aguleri is the eldest son of Eri. Nri people before crowning their Eze (ruler) come to Aguleri to consult with and make sacrifices to the important idols of Aguleri, obtain approval and receive "Udulu Eze" from Aguleri. (Idigo, M.C.M; 1965 P.73).

This is a further deviation from the "truth" since Anadi in his work affirmed the founder and father of Aguleri as Agulu-Nnamenyi, whereas, he posited Menri as the second son and founder of other tribes. This goes ahead to establish that many more studies and investigations are yet to be carried on the history of Umueri and not just building baseless castle and proclaiming it as the history and origin of the entire Igbo. According to most of the versions on Aguleri tradition, the Umueri were originally of Igala stock and have a fanciful tale on how they eventually dispersed and Onoja the son of the second wife founded the community at Idah, which later became the Igala while the children of the first wife founded the Eri lineages as they exist today among Igbo communities.

Emmanuel Ifesieh, in his compilation on the Eri tradition supported the view of Anadi on Menri being the second son but ironically could not establish the origin of the kingship he vested on him.

> Umueri tradition of origin maintain that Menri, the second son of Eri left his natal home at Aguleri with 'Ofo', 'Alo' and 'Adama' and settled temporarily at Mkpume Onyilenyi, the present site of Enugwu-Ukwu. There, he was 'considered' the divine king-Eze Nri II and bore the children…Under divine inspiration, he sensed that his end was close and like a real, holy and an orthodox traditional ruler, summoned Ifiukwuanim and Namoko and with the ritual powers invested on him, he passed on his spirit to them, by placing their hands together on the sacred symbols of 'Ofo' and 'Alo' Nri-Eri and declared them and their descendants perpetual divine kings, and that from them alone should Eze Nri-Eri be selected. (Ifesieh E.I 1989 p.68).

One would have naturally most expected a crisis somewhere on the lineage that introduced the dual kingship. Also, if Menri were correctly the second son of Eri, one would also expect that an explanation be given about the displacement of the first son. It is not unnatural that such a situation might arise as with the case of Esau and Jacob in the Bible but there must be some significant event that would put a spark to it. Ifesieh went ahead to write that:

> This in effect meant that from then, there was a creation of dual Nri dynasties. Ifiukwuanims line at Agukwu and Namoko who succeeded him as the "I Eze-Nri king with his line at Oraeri (Ora-Eri). Ifiukwuanim bore the following children: Agbadana or Umu Onyiora, Uruoji or Umu-Alikenri, Obeagu or Umu-Nribuife. Nri Namoko's residence was near the Agulu Lake where he bore the following children; Ozu, the father of Umu-Eri (which is now a part of Neni town), Diodo, the father of Umu-Diodo (now part of Akamkpisi in Agukwu-Nri) and Ovolo, the father of the present Mba-Ukwu and Umuona. (Ifesieh E.I, P.69)

Significantly, this part where Nri Namoko and his children lived near the Agulu lake is yet untouched. Research has not succeeded in finding anything or objects on this spot that will link this culture to the Igbo-Ukwu culture (Archeology). In fact, history has it that after the crises that introduced this dual kingship, the other kingship lineage fled to Adazi-Enu where they were welcomed as 'nwadiana' because their mother came from this community. They were eventually settled at Nnokwa. Later Avo collected the insignia of office and migrated to Oraeri near Igbo-Ukwu and found the dynasty there. The subsequent towns created by other Eri lineage are very small group of peoples making small towns or villages or a part of other towns. How then to account for the rest of the massive Igbo kingdom remain an enigma to Eri culture adherents. However, neither of the two sites of Eri kingship nor other subsequent settlements have any evidence of long or continued occupation.

Avo, the father of Oraeri received his kingship through his father Namoko in spite of being one of the last. This is expected since it is said that Avo served him so well. The history goes that when Namoko became very old and weak, he called Avo, invoked the great God-Chukwu to rain down his blessings on Avo. He gave him the Ofo-Nri-Eri and the Alo-Nri, as empirical ritual staffs of his sacred office and finally gave him the pectoral mask called Nwata Ona worn around the neck by the Eze-Nri-Eri of Ora-Eri. Study the similarities between these pendants and compare them with these Igbo-ukwu pendants.

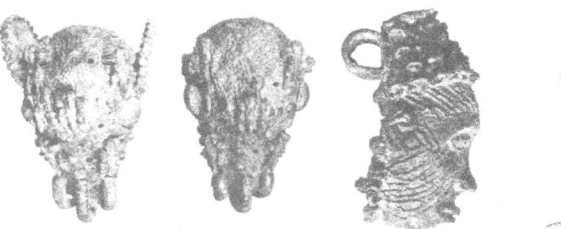

Some Igbo-Ukwu bronze pendant

Benin Ivory Pendant 6.5inches

The Pectoral Mask worn by Eze Nri of Ora-Eri (Nwata Ona) 6.25inches

Significantly, this "Nwata Ona" and the other empirical ritual staffs given to Avo are surviving up till date. Also, none of the other materials were made of bronze or in any pattern that will relate them to the Igbo-Ukwu bronzes. The pectoral mask or Nwata Ona does not even bear the Ichi mark seen on the faces of the finds at Igbo-Ukwu and analysis show that it is Benin Bronze of the 14th century.

Again, Namoko blessed the Adama (Eze-Nri's ritual priest) and advised them to leave in search of a new home after his death because he was afraid that Avo's brother might kill him when their father died. At the death of Namoko, Avo collected the sacred symbols given to him by his father and left with Adama and Nnokwa-Ike, the younger brother who later became the founder of Nnokwa. They moved off to Oraeri where they established Nri theocracy. History also has it that on arrival, Avo took the title of Nri and became the reigning Eze-Nri of Oraeri. Avo also went to pick a wife from Igbo (Igbo-Ukwu), which is just a mile from their present settlement. This goes to explain also that people already occupied this area before the advent of Avo and his brothers. Again, it was never proved that Avo founded any great kingdom apart from being a mere saprophyte which found itself protected under the protectorate of Igbo (Igbo-Ukwu). In fact, the manners in which the history of Eri and the lineages as, told by the adherents, include references to other towns say all about the subservience of the culture to the real Igbo culture. If Eri had any hegemony on the Igbo speaking area or any political power to count on as portrayed by the kingship structure, how was it that just a village in Igbo-Ukwu could drive them back in war? Why was he unable to use his influence, if there was any, to organize militia from other areas where he controlled? The nature of Eri influence as claimed by the adherents ought therefore to be re-examined.

According to Ora-Eri tradition of origin, the first Eze-Nri and his successors to date are as follows:

1st	*Eri Eze-Nri I*
2nd	*Menri Eze-Eri II who consecrated his sons as*
	Next Eze Nri, as noted earlier. Two separate
	Dynasties, Ora-Eri and Agukwu came into
	Being. Namoko was responsible for Ora-Eri line, while
	Ifukwuanim is for Agukwu.
3rd	*Namoko-Eze-Nri III*
4th	*Avo Eze-Nri IV*
5th	*Nriagu Eze-Nri V*
6th	*Nnokwa Eze-Nri VI*
7th	*Bike Eze-Nri VII*
8th	*Ochife Eze-Nri VII*
9th	*Ezulu Eze-Nri IX*
10th	*Ochife Eze-Nri X*
11th	*Ezegwo Eze-Nri XI*
12th	*Ofia Eze-Nri XII*

13th   *Okubalu Eze-Nri XIII*
14th   *Ezudemba Eze-Nri XIV*
15th   *Ezenwosu Eze-Nri XV*
16th   *Ezizundu Eze-Nri XVI*
17th   *Abraham Ezeokonkwo Eze-Nri XVII*
18th   *Joe-M.C.Obiakor Eze-Nri XVIII*

(Ifesieh, 1989 P.68.)

This attempt by Ifesieh to recount the past Eze-Nri of Oraeri may not be far from the truth. Since it is consistent with other attempts especially on the number, which is approximately equal to the number of Eze-Nri on the other dynasty at Agukwu. It at least proves the dynasties to exist parallel at the same interval of time.

At Agukwu, Northcote Thomas, an English anthropologist who worked on the Nri people in the early part of this century recorded also 18 Eze-Nris'at Agukwu.

1st   *Nri Namoko*
2nd   *Nri Bife*
3rd   *Nri Fenenu*
4th   *Nri Ainyaboa*
5th   *Nri Jimofor*
6th   *Nri Apia*
7th   *Nri Alikenri*
8th   *Nri Anyamata*
9th   *Nri Omalo*
10th *Nri Ezono*
11th *Nri Ago*
12th *Nri Okbakbo*
13th *Nri Omalonoinyaso*
14th *Nri Ifikanum*
15th *Nri Evuzo*
16th *Nri Ewenata*

17th   Nri Ezimilo
18th   Nri Akike (now living)
          (Northcote Thomas; 1913 P.49-50)

Though significantly, he omitted Ifiukwanim, Menri and Eri and posited Namoko as the beginning of the lineage. Also, the spelling of the name may not be accurate. It may not be clearly said between his work and Onwuejeogwu's work, which is nearer to the truth since Onwuejeogwu's work was at a very later day. He has his record as follows:

1st   Nri Ifiukwuanim
2nd   Nri Namoko
3rd   Nri Buife
4th   (name forgotten)
5th   Nri Nrijiofor
6th   Nri (name forgotten)
7th   Nri Anyamata
8th   Nri Fenenu
9th   Nri Agu
10th   Nri Alike and Nri Apia
11th   Nri Ezimilo
12th   Nri Ewenetem
13th   Nri Enweleana
14th   Nri Obalike
15th   Nri Nrijiofor II
          (Onwuejeogwu, M.A.; 1981 P.25)

In as much as we consider the fact that the account was bound to be thinner as time went by, we shall also believe that these accounts are not very far from the truth, at least for their consistency in number. However, speculating on dates from our knowledge of such chronology does not carry us beyond the 16th century, for the existence of Oraeri. Counting from Avo who was the founder of Oraeri, we count a total of 14 kings. Making an extra over estimate of 50years for the reign of each king, which is only supernaturally possible, it carries us only to the 14th century of the existence of Avo. How then do we reconcile such a culture with a culture that is probably on the decline in the 9th century? It beats the imagination how Onwuejeogwu was able to assign the dates A.D.948 to 1041 to the Eri culture. It is glaring, the difficulties that he met in assigning dates because of his inconsistency and unreality. Perhaps the reason for his getting locked in ambiguities was for his effort to tie this culture with the Igbo-Ukwu culture. Other scholars who have done more realistic work on the dating of Eri migration such as Idigo affirm that Eri migrated from Igala to Aguleri about 400 years ago. Besides, the Igala kingship, which Eri claim to be related to either by descent or by consanguinity has never been dated by historians and anthropologists as being older than 1600A.D. The period of Eri kingship cannot be older than that of Igala.

Surprisingly, the towns and lineages that have something to do with the word "Igbo" do not make any claim on this culture but Eri lineages, which have nothing to do with "Igbo", do. Towns like Aguleri, Umuleri, Oraeri, Agukwu-Nri etc. speak nothing about "Igbo" but "Eri". The Igbo culture, which will not give a name without reason has some town names as 'Igbo-Ukwu' (The great Igbo), purely and simply called "Igbo" before 1942 when the suffix "Ukwu" was added. Others include 'Igbo-Etiti' (The central Igbo), Igbo-Uzo (On the way Igbo), 'Ama-Igbo' (The Shore of the Igbo), 'Obi-Igbo' (The heart or home of the Igbo) 'Okpala-Igbo (The head or the first son of the Igbo), 'Azu-Igbo' (The back of Igbo), 'Igbo-Eze' (The kingly Igbo), Aro-Oke-Igbo etc. Unfortunately, none of these communities or lineages makes any claim on the Igbo culture. It beats the imagination why the Eri lineages make this claim, when they are clearly not that Igbo. Eri culture adherents have in actual fact clearly delineated and demarcated the ancestors and descendants of Eri from the rest of Igbo.

Jeffreys in his work on the Nri people was able to affirm, "Though these people speak only Igbo, they declare that they are not Igbo (Jeffrey; 1935 P.346). He continued in his research to find from the people that they are brothers to the Igala, concluding that they were either an offshoot of the Igala or that they, Umueri, and the Igala derived from a common stock". (Jeffrey 1935 P.271).

Moreover, the account of the Umueri culture only limits us to the knowledge of Agukwu, Amanuke, Igbariam, Enugwu Ukwu, Aguleri, Oraeri and other kindred of the lineage in Igboland. This is just less than 1/50 of what the entire Igbo race is and little does this establish any connection or links between the other parts of Igboland and Eri culture. If the other Igbo came from a different stock, as this culture tends to establish, then the result would have been that the minority would have to disappear in the cultural conflict that would ensue. Some part of the Igbo, just as they allowed the political and economic dominance of the Aro, only allowed the religious dominance of the Umueri just as the Jews did to the Levites. Umueri who were and who are the weaker minority could not have enforced their culture on the majority. The situation could be that cultures already in existence in these places were in their wane and only gained revival from the Umueri or something else should come to explain these riddles. That the Umueri were allowed the priestly role of saying prayers before the breaking of kola nut, make offering, amend sacrifices and undertake burials which are not meant to be carried out by a son of the soil as in the case of Okonkwo's suicide in "Things Fall Apart" does not form a basis for the claim on the Igbo aboriginals.

The claim of Nri as the cultural center of the Igbo is based on their claim to be the first to arrive at this part whereas Aguleri could as well be understood to be the cultural center based on his being the first son. The extent of the validity of these claims still lies undisclosed.

> At the time of Nri's arrival in this part of the world, there were no other towns in the immediate vicinity, nothing but one country and so the settlement was called Agukwu meaning the great field. (Isichei, E.A; 1926 P.4)

Ordinarily 'Agu-Ukwu' should not be the name of a person but the descriptive name of a place. The common meaning is a large space away from inhabited areas. On another hand if 'Agu-Ukwu' were to be the name of a person then it would have been a praise name or a title and the meaning will be 'The great lion'.

Those who hold to the Nri origin of the Igbo often support their claims by stating that Nri priest went all round, through the whole Igboland giving ofo to enable them to take the Ozo title.

> The religious influence of Nri once extended over the whole of Igbo country. The Nri were the high priests of the idols and from their hands the Chiefs loved to receive their insignia of office. (Jordan, J.P; 1975 P.41).

However, it is clearly on record about the extent of influence of the Eri culture in Igboland. In spite of the much exaggeration made to this already, we know that:

> The Eze Nri kings of Oraeri and Agukwu had well instituted paths of travel during their ritual missions to other Igbo communities. The Ora-Eri Eze-Nri passed through Adazi, Nnokwa, Nnobi, Ojoto, Agbaja, Oba, Obosi, and Onitsha etc. and reached its zenith with the ritual passage and sacrifice to the lordly Niger. The Nze-Nri of Agukwu passed through Enugwu-Ukwu, Abagana, Ukpo, Awkuzu, Nteje, Umuleri and Aguleri etc. where he normally *got a lump of clay from Anambra River. (Ifesieh E.I; P.79).*

I have purposely chosen to take this citation from the work of one of the revered sons of Oraeri on Eri culture. So we now know very well from this that Eri cultural influence did not extend beyond the children of Eri and the neighbouring territory. This given area of influence precisely along Anambra River can only account for just a little fragment of what the Igbo are. This is why so many other Igbo spread through the language tribe, like people from Orlu, Owerri, Mbaise, Nsukka, Abakaliki, Enugu, Okigwe etc. often got annoyed at the projection of the Eri culture as a culture that binds the Igbo. This is because they know little about this culture. They only know about Igbo and nothing but Igbo culture, which they know they belong to and are a part of.

It is true also that because some Igbo communities believed in religious superiority of the Eri, they invited the great medicine men from Eri to install gods for them. Kings, wealthy and titled men believed that the best protective charms and amulets (of power) came from Eri. They go to the Eri priests to procure such charms but the number of communities that involved in this act and the extent to which this culture diffused into Igboland then were scanty. The Ofo for instance is now widely accepted but only to take the place of 'Ogu' that has been or existed parallel with it.

The 'Ofo' and other cultures introduced by the Nri is only a fragment of the Igbo cultures. That some parts of the Igbo accepted the superiority of some of the religious cultures of the Nri is simply a path towards the march of culture change. This is in every nook natural and proves the Igbo culture to be resilient and not altogether ejective of other cultural influence. The process I would most describe as the additive process of culture change, where new elements are accepted, not to replace existing ones but added to them without introducing crisis or conflict of values.

Recognizing that the Umueri tradition is much older than the Umunri tradition and that the latter is related to the former in the second degree will help in the process of reconciling the two traditions. In the same vein, we realize that these two cultures are not situated beyond the 16th century. On the other hand, the exclusivity of the entire Igbo race in this cultural account and particularly from the origin and the lack of any use of the word 'Igbo' show this culture to be far more secondary or separate from, the Igbo culture.

> Nri left Aguleri and migrated southwards into Igboland and established the Nri theocratic hegemony in the present Nri town. (Onwuejeogwu M.A).

From these words from Michael Onwuejeogwu's Odinani, one can correctly infer that already, there exists a land called Igboland into which the Nri migrated. From my exposition in the early chapter of this work, it was proved that kingdoms and peoples migrate in Africa because of the abundance of land. However, such migrations do not at the same time account for the cultural change which either comes from within or from without. Onwuejeogwu's work affirmed that people existed here before the arrival of Eri but he did not explain the origin of these people. These people whom are identified as the Adama and the Nsekpe have their origins left verbose. History shows that these people are the aboriginal stock at Aguleri and are regarded as the original owners of the land as well as the ritual and political head of the entire Nri settlement. The Adama also formed the Umudiana kindred in Ekwenanyika village of Akamkpisi. The Adama and Nsekpe are not related to Eri by origin.

One also begins to wonder from the mythology how blacksmith sent by Chukwu with his bellows was able to dry the land and from where the blacksmith came. Most importantly, as we can understand from the mythology that Eri rewarded him with 'Ofo' and had him settled at Awka, one cannot see reason why the Awka is not included among the lineages of Eri or at least get Awka established as another principal origin of Igbo. Perhaps, Awka may be one of the Igbo communities that gave a helping hand to the Eri at their arrival and got their 'Ofo' culture in return. As we know, blacksmithing is not only seen in Awka today in Igboland but in several other places where the culture has earlier diffused.

Again, the famous Odinani talks of the Nri priests moving from village to village carrying in their hands the staff of political and ritual authority. Also, many towns for prestige and political reasons associated themselves with Nri calling themselves the children of Eri (Umueri). Such statement only carries us further to a stronger foundation of making conclusions. It is clear that the priests only sort to extend their religious influence to places where they did not exist, therefore, making this culture peculiar to Nri and not Igbo. The move to associate with Nri also take us to believing that the Nri were sometimes not one of the Igbo until lately which is contained in the findings of Jeffrey's.

The recent excavations made in Igbo-Ukwu, which dated back to the 9th century by carbon dating, make us understand that people have lived in this land long before the advent of the Aro or the Nri. It is also more logical that we should know very little of this culture because of the time difference (age) since the further we go back to history, the thinner the records become. The difficulty in tracing this lineage would not make us go down into accepting secondary facts because they are clearer in our heads. This also reveals that the knowledge of Ironwork was not new in Igboland

"We can know only certain aspects of a vanished civilization and the older the civilization; the fewer are those aspects since we can only have knowledge of things which have survived the assault of time. There is therefore a tendency to take the part for the whole and to conclude that since certain aspects of the two civilizations (one contemporary and the other lost in the past) show similarities, there must be resemblance in all aspect. Not only is this reasoning logically indefensible in many cases, it is actually refuted by the facts"(Levi Straus). This is one of the important mistakes which Onwuejeogwu had made while trying to claim the artifacts from Igbo-Ukwu as Nri'.

The Nri only laid a claim to the finds at Igbo-Ukwu because of the discovery of the 'Ichi' mark on some of the human faces found among the finds. Significantly, there is a very big deviation or variance between the pattern of the mark which spread around the face with lines concentric at the bridge of the nose and that seen on the face of the Eze-Nri designate of Oraeri, Chief Obijekwe, as they appear on page 71 of E. Ifesieh's work: Religion at the Grassroots.

Significantly also, the earlier Eze-Nri in the same work does not have the mark on their faces, showing that this culture is not Eri tradition. It is proper to put it here that it is not only in Nri and other Eri kingdoms that the Ichi mark is found. The 'Ichi' scarification art belongs to the Umudioka and not the Umueri. Moreover, the figure having the Ichi on the bronze stand is the figure of a woman whereas; Eri culture prohibits a woman from taking the 'Ichi' marks except the first daughter of an Eri king. Jeffreys (1951 pg. 93) discovered that 'among Awgwu people, both men and women received the 'Ichi' mark. This together with the picture of the daughter of Umeorizu of Igbo-Ukwu who bear the same 'Ichi' mark, go a long way to prove that this is a culture in decline and which has been borrowed with misconception and aberrations from the real thing.

Moreover, the Igala where the Eri claim to have their origin has not the 'Ichi' culture. The Igala do not possess any religious affiliation to the python or the tortoise, which are mortises found in the Igbo-Ukwu culture and which has religious inclinations in most parts of Igboland. Why should the adherents of Eri culture clinch on these as factors that link the Igbo-Ukwu culture with the Eri.

The 'Ichi' as we know is a painful blood bond taken usually by young men and women. This binds them to the community and makes them a full-fledged and responsible citizen of that community. On the other hand, there exist another kind of 'Ichi' given usually to slaves and immigrants. This 'Ichi' is also a bond, binding them to the community in which they have settled and which sets them as free citizens of the community. Such bonds prevent them from doing any harm to any member of the community or working against the community at large. However, the pattern of such 'Ichi' is different from that taken by the freeborn citizens. Perhaps, this is the kind of 'Ichi' seen on the faces of the Eri people. Many of the Eri sons still bear this mark today. Perhaps, because of what it means to they and they have conventionally adopted it as their own culture, while the archetype of this culture is already disappearing. However, the archetype of this culture could still be found on the faces of many old men.

The bronze Altar Stand from Igbo-Ukwu with a figure of a woman with an ichi mark on the face Marking that occur on the Igbo-Ukwu Bronzes
Source: Shaw 1977

Again, the fact that Igbo do not give a name without some meaning or aim in view will leave us with yet a lot to study about the origin of the names of such town like Ichi, Amichi, and Ichida etc. More claims may still come on this culture if people would actually give time to this study. Umudioka as is still very alive in the memory is the last town where 'Ichi' carving experts lived. Their pattern of 'Ichi' known, as the 'Ichi Umudioka' remains closer to the 'Ichi' of Igbo-Ukwu finds. This again leaves us with wider arena of inquiry.

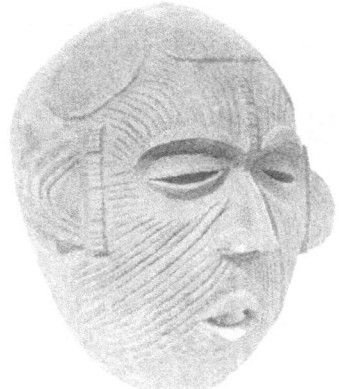

Nwa Ndibi, a wooden mask obtained from the Udi division, and showing the same type of facial marks.
Source: Shaw 1977

It has been proved that the Eri culture did not diffuse any distance in Igboland. A man from Udi area will tell you that he knew nothing of the Eri culture but that he is an Igbo man. The discovery of Nwandibi from Udi area, which is today lying in the Lagos museum, should divert our thoughts completely. A close inspection of the Nwandibi will reveal the same pattern of 'Ichi' mark, which is concentric on the bridge of the nose, similar to the one in the Igbo-Ukwu finds. This reveals that the culture in Igbo-Ukwu has in more primitive time diffused into this area from Igbo-Ukwu. Notice also that such culture was also in decline in the area along with the decline of the Igbo-Ukwu culture putting the two cultures into the same cultural tradition. However, the Ichi of the Nri is quite a different thing with lots of aberrations and was only in the rise when the real culture was in its wane. This calls for a thorough study of those finds which should be the primary concern of Igbo rather than making hair-splitting arguments on who claims the finds. As we shall see in other chapters of this work, these finds have a lot to reveal about the Igbo.

Likewise, the 'Nwata Ona' should not be presumed to be related to the pectoral pendants found at Igbo-Ukwu since many traditional titled men around the area of Igbo and even beyond can produce such pendants and even those closer to that of Igbo-Ukwu. Several cultures have their priesthood and kingship regalia, which hardly exclude such pendants. We can make a case study of the Bini or Nok culture. Appearance of such similar materials or artifacts would not be the basis for relating any two cultures. Moreover, the 'Nwata Ona' even though made of bronze, is not in any pattern to relate it to Igbo-Ukwu finds. Also, 'Nwata Ona' has not the 'Ichi' mark as seen in some of the pendants, neither is its components Igbo-Ukwu bronzes. In fact, the archeologist Thurstan Shaw who saw and studied it called it the Benin Bronze of 14th century. (Thurstan Shaw; 1977)

Again, we are aware of the fact that the Igbo knew no kings (Igbo ama eze). It beats the imagination therefore, how it has been possible to talk of the Eze-Nri Agukwu and Eze-Nri-Oraeri. There is no confusion about this, since this is Eri culture and not Igbo culture as in Igbo culture, there are no kings. The proposition of Obiechina that this is only a figure of speech lies on the narrowness of thought in treating the modern Igbo society in isolation of the ancient Igbo society. Nowadays, so many, if not all Igbo communities have made attempt to fall into the modern tune of society by enacting kings. Clearly, this has almost everywhere in Igboland proved a failure since it has not been easy for many communities to raise a single king.

Perhaps, Igbo receptivity to change has brought about these deformities. A visitor to Igboland will be surprised at the number of chiefs one finds everywhere. This phenomenon is not more than 20 years old and owes its origin to the acceptance of the warrant chieftaincy culture introduced by Europeans. Chiefs sprouted like mushrooms throughout Igbo land and as Chinua writes; " From having no kings in their recent past, the Igbo swung round to set an all-time record of four hundred kings in Imo and four hundred in Anambra. Most of them are traders in their stall by day and monarchs at night, city dwellers five days a week and traditional rulers on Saturday and Sundays. They adopted traditional robes from every land, including, I am told, the ceremonial regalia of the Lord Mayor of London" (Achebe; "The Trouble with Nigeria", Enugu, Fourth Dimension. 1983 P.48)

Igbo only naturally recognize wealthy nobles and accord them the rights of kings according to one's achievements, rights like ritual burial exhumed in the bowels of Igbo-Ukwu. Eri, for their kingship culture should not be Igbo in the real sense.

The Aro that came from the same stock as the Ibibio could not have been influenced to adopt common characteristics as the Nri who came from the same stock as Igala all by an accident. Likewise are other cultures of migration. There must have existed some aboriginal stock that rendered a common influence on these different sets of people. This therefore presents us with complexities and we are aware of how uneasy it is to tie the Igbo culture to entirely one center or to one tradition. This is because a cultural center may combine two or more or all these traditions. Being aware of this, the task now becomes what are the most primitive elements and the principal and most influential settlers. Where was this prehistoric settlement?

Ezechima Culture

A Critical Overview of a Brief History of Ezechima Clan

(*A bulk of this part is taken from 'Igbo Kingdoms' written by Professor Lambert U. Ejiofor*)

Ejiofor defended a doctorate thesis on the Igbo kingdom, power and control in which he raised fundamental questions about the pattern of Igbo migration by a groundwork study of the Ezechima clan. He also opened a great light on the traditional political system of the people, which for the direct and indirect foreign influence on it almost assumed a chameleonic outlook. He made a thorough research and critical overview of both the oral, written and empirical data in this study that perhaps, no one can add any better words.

He talked of two major versions of the origin of this people. The first and more disseminated is that they emigrated from Benin and were by implication of Edo stock. The second which is more restricted but well reasoned is that they migrated from the East of the Niger, pushed into the western region and later pulled back to their present position. Oral history is strong in its support of the first, while a second look at events and correlation of factors would strengthen the second version.

According to Ejiofor, eminent scholars like Dr. Nnamdi Azikiwe, Professor Ikenna Azimiro and Professor Elizabeth Isichei support the Benin origin. Some scholars born in the area such as Lawrence Okpuno, S.I Bosah, P.O. Nwaobi and Charles U. Diei reinforce them. A galaxy of oral informants also maintained the Bini descent but they disagree on details, chronology and particular characters and pattern of migration.

There were some upheavals in the Bini kingdom during the 16th century. A particular man or group who was supposed to be the father of Umuezechima disagreed with the reigning king and was forced out of Benin. Nzimiro relates that "Onitsha oral history begins with the myths of the Umuezechima clan, who trace their ancestry to Chima, the great father who lived at Ado N' idu (Benin). The name "Chima" is generally a woman's name among the Igbo. This is arguable and in-fact is not true, but previous scholars on this topic like Charles Diei alludes to this notion when he wrote;" One source has it that Chima was the only daughter of a certain Benin Oba (probably Ozolua) who at the point of death, feared that his people would riot if he named Chima his successor since never in the annals of history was a woman known to wear the Benin crown (Diei C.U; 1974, P.1)

The name alone cannot explain much. Chima is one of those Igbo names that are used for either sex like Ngozi, Uchenna and Chika. Diei made a similar point when he noted that "a critical look at this source reveals that it does not seem to be authentic", although his explanation cannot be accepted with any stroke of finality. There is no authority to persuade one that "the word "Chima" in Igbo language is not the name of a woman but a man. Moreover, the prefix "Eze" in Igbo language means king or natural ruler. It is therefore very unlikely that Chima was a different person from Eze".

This leads to the second question - Chima (another version of Chukwuma) is an authentic Igbo name, which is used freely in all Igbo sub-cultural areas, many of which did not come under Benin rule. What explanation does one offer for a Bini bearing a typical Igbo name? One may of course postulate a theory of lexical evolution or suggest that Chima need not necessarily be a fugitive from Benin. One can only suggest in the face of oral and written persuasions, that the burden is on the claimant to prove their case and that Chima remains Igbo until the reverse is proved. The Benin tradition has it that Chima was a great warrior and was probably at the head of a farming group in Benin. He later had a dispute with Esigie, the mother of the Oba of Benin who was insulted and assaulted because she had trespassed on his farmland. As a reprisal, the Oba sent his military chief Obugwala to attack Chima and this led to a civil war, which rent the Benin kingdom. At this stage, a few problems arose. Elizabeth Isichei writes that the ruler of Benin himself was Oba Esigie (c.1517-c.1550). It is unlikely that he would bear the same name as his mother. However, Dr. Azikiwe qualifies the name within acceptable uncertainty. He called the woman "Queen Esigie" which leaves two interpretations open; she could be the Queen as mother and that would dispute "Esigie" unless the reigning Esigie was the second or later of that name, or she could be the wife of Oba Esigie and that could justify her answering to that name.

According to Bosah, "the name of the queen (mother) could not have been Esigie since the ruling monarch at the time of the flight was himself, Esigie. His mother therefore could not have borne an identical name. In-fact, her name was Idia. Her title was Lyaba (Queen mother)". He equally questioned the authenticity of Obugwala (or Aguala) military expeditions against Chima and his group. He thinks that he was a mistaken identity for Oguala who was regarded as the wisest Oba of Benin, having caused a trench to be dug around the town in which he resided and thus protected it from invasion. By this act, the town later became known as Benin City. Oba Oguala reigned in the closing period of the thirteenth century.

The second question revolves around the circumstances of the supposed flight. If the Oba of Benin was such a powerful monarch, how could Chima have organised such a fateful insurrection against him because of a relatively flimsy reason of trespass on farmland? If the salience of the issue is tendered to explain the aggravation, how does one defend the view that Chima was a son of the royal house mutinied so unrepentantly? These puzzles have no immediate explanations. Whether it was

Chima or his ancestors, all in the Benin traditions agree that there was the great trek eastwards.

The pattern of the trek becomes undecided. An elaborate account by Bosah has it that the emigrants first rested at Azara Agogoro for a few days and later arrived Agbor where they domiciled for several years during which they lived with Ibo speaking people and started to lose their original language and part of their cultural mode of life redolent with Benin. It is quite striking that the language of the dominant culture could be lost to their neighbours in transit, more so when those neighbours were part of the great Benin empire. The march continued, apparently led by Chima, until it settled in the present Ezechima clan area. At this point, narratives part ways.

A strong tradition led by Bosah tells us that Obor was the first place of settlement and that from there, some of the emigrants moved into Onicha-Ugbo, Onicha-Ukwu, Onicha Olona and Onitsha east of the Niger. The others moved into Issele Uku out of which grew Issele Azagba and Issele Mkpitime, while Obomkpa and Ezi sprang up under the same circumstances. Bosah includes Ulah and Ibusa in the genealogical chart, but Onwuejeogwu would immediately exclude Ibusa from the story, for he holds emphatically that Ibusa was founded by emigrants from Isu and Nri, east of the Niger (Onwuejeogwu M.A; 1972 P.6)

The overwhelming evidence of oral tradition in the area shows that the sons of Chima founded the communities in Ezechima clan. Azikiwe's account suggests however, that the main destination of the emigration as east of the Niger and it was "some who did not have the stout heart of the pioneer warriors" that "decided to settle at different places known today as Onicha Olona, Onitsha Mili, Obor, Issele Uku..." (Azikiwe N; 1970 P.12). Isichei puts it simply by stating " this migration moved through western Iboland towards the Niger, founding enroute the towns known collectively as Umuezechima (Isichei E; 1973 P.39).

The Benin origin of Umuezechima is questioned seriously in another tradition. Leading challenges in the non-Benin traditions includes eminent scholars like A.E. Afigbo, M.A. Onwuejeogwu and to at least, an indirect extent, Elizabeth Isichei. Tracing the pattern of Igbo migration, Afigbo wrote on the western Igbo, among others:

"An analysis of this would indicate that the Western Igbo left Nri-Awka area and crossed the humid and waterlogged Anambra Niger flood plain to occupy the uplands stretching from Asaba to Agbor. On running into the Edo to the West, the tip of this migration would appear to have been blunted. One result of this was the settlement of the southern Ika and the River line Igbo area around Aboh. The other result was that some of the group which had gone farthest West traced their steps Eastwards. Some of them in fact, re-crossed the Niger and settled at Onitsha. Some of those involved in this recoil constitute the …Ezechima group…(Afigbo in Igbo Language and Culture; 1975 P.39).

The extent of the homogeneity of the Igbo group which extend to Umuezechima clan and the similarity in customs and lexical identity between the Nri-Awka Igbo and the Umuezechima Igbo are strong arguments in defense of Afigbo's postulations. The accepted presence of Nri element among the population west of the Niger, particularly the Ogboli quarters in Issele Uku, further strengthens their traditions. Even the minor linguistic dissimilarity, which distinguishes the various sub cultural groups among the Igbo, was not strikingly noticed during this research. Dialogue was easy and free. Particularly, at Onicha Olona, one man noted at the Iyase's house, that the researcher behaved as if he was born in Ezechima, for the traditional courtesy gestures and proverbial expressions were practically identical. There is such a close affinity in cultural traits that it would be forcing the matter to try to prove that there is a genealogical link. Perhaps, this research might start another train of thought on the migrations for nothing spectacular would rule out distant possibilities of Igbo migrating from the west to the east. However, it is left to some scholars who will be up to the titanic task of establishing this historical tradition to initiate this trend. They will need to adduce strong argument for the movement of a majority group from the lavishly fertile plains of the west of the Niger.

At this point, we begin to admit possibilities. " It could be sustained that the Ezechima Igbo emigrated from Benin in a backward thrust when the tip of this emigration would appear to have blunted" (Afigbo; 1972). Nothing eliminates at least in theory, the chances of the Igbo moving westwards only to be repulsed by the reverses of fortune. Elizabeth Isichei pressingly referred to it when she noted; "Chima and his followers may well have been Igbo as Chima's own name suggests. Various versions of traditions suggest that either they were Igbo brought as slaves or hostages to the Benin court, or coming from a homeland in Western Igboland". (Isichei E; 1975).

This seems to come to term with Onwuejeogwu's contribution; " Evidence from other sources shows that Chima was a runaway from Agbor and cannot see why Benin oral tradition is completely silent about the Chima episode" (Onwuejeogwu; 1972 P.33).

There is no contradiction between Agbor and Benin hypotheses. The former is about 60km east of the later, and nothing stops the migration from taking off from Benin and sojourning in Agbor for so immemorial a duration that Benin oral tradition would lose grip with the episode, which might tally with Bosah's earlier account. Nevertheless, the suggestion that the immigrants were originally Igbo has not been defeated.

From the evidence before us, the following may be upheld. Chima must have founded Ezechima clan of which the nine communities mentioned above are definitely components. There was migration either directly or indirectly from Agbor. There is no compelling reason to reject migration from Benin, as there is every reason to accept a first migration to or towards Benin. The immigrants must have been Igbo. The lexical and cultural connections between Ezechima Igbo and other Igbo people east of the Niger are so close that it is farfetched to excise them from Igbo genealogy. Finally, the geographical location of Ezechima communities amidst the other Igbo from Agbor to Asaba and from Ogwashi Uku and Ubulu-Uku to Illah seems an unnatural jump in the pattern of migration.

However, some elites of Ezechima base their claim of Benin descent on the similarity between their traditional political structure and those of Benin. However, this could be explained in other ways. First, the Benin Empire is said to have once extended to the Niger, if not beyond. An expansionist Oba ruled Benin in the fifteenth century.

"In the heydays, the boundaries of the Benin State stretched beyond its solid core, taking little account of linguistic and cultural divides. The kingdom was bounded by the Yoruba speakers on the west and north, Ibo on the east, Ishan, and Northern Edo on the north west and Urhobo, Itsekiri and Ijaw on the south" (Forde, D and Kaberry P.M; 1976 P.5).

It would be almost unnatural if groups, which were for considerable duration under Benin imperial administration, did not reflect the facts and styles of that administration. In the absence of colonial control, such group could be held together only by a centralized monarchy. Ezechima communities have copied the monarchy and centralized administration. Nzimiro notes that "the founders established the Benin type of kingship and went to the Oba of Benin to receive the sword of office known as ada: hence I style them the ada kings, for example, the Onicha, Issele, and other Umuezechima towns of Asaba division" (Ikenna Nzimiro; P.8).

The Obi in an Umuezechima community takes pride in his historical connections with the Oba of Benin and to date strives to have the Oba or his representative present at his coronation. The Obi of Issele-Uku emphasized that he had to receive his ada from the oba or his representative and that the beaded crown was a carry-over of the Benin royal tradition. The Obi of Ezi also wears the beaded crown.

One may compare the Benin presence to the presence of the Nri Priest at the ritual initiation of people into the Ozo title and at some royal coronation. In fact, at Issele-Uku, the Onisha who crowns the Obi is always from the Ogboli quarters or Nri descent. In the past, those Igbo groups who exercised extensive influence helped to shape the culture of many other groups. If the early Portuguese maps extended the eastern frontier of Benin rule beyond the Niger to Bonny, it was only logical that the ruling dynasties of most of the western Igbo Chiefdom should claim Benin origin and their title systems modeled after Benin"(Bradbury R.E; 1970 P.22).

Bradbury notes immediately "in recent centuries, the recognition of the Oni of Ife's spiritual seniority over the Oba appears to have no political implications. Be this as it may, it can only be expected that given Igbo receptivity to change, the political system of the western Igbo communities should bear some evidence of Benin contacts. The inter-mixture of Igbo language with some Yoruba and Benin words as was pointed out by Bosah could be interpreted as legacies of long association.

The Igbo-Ukwu Culture

(Most of this part is taken from the unpublished works of Sir S. B. Obikwelu.)

It is quite unfortunate that some writers on Igbo-Ukwu culture write on the periphery, thereby failing to examine the true crux of the matter. Some of these writers depend on hearsay and solely on what foreigners had written on our archeological remains. Not many of them have gone into this all-important event on the life of Igbo man with a true sense of dedication by making a down to earth research through establishing personal contacts with the inhabitants of the area the excavations were made. A development of such great significance, which has enabled the Igbo man to achieve a legitimate place of honour in the verdict of history, ought to be handled with a true sense of mission. It should be the joint responsibility of many historians to project the identity Igbo-Ukwu culture has given the Igbo man in the context of the black race to the outside world. There is no doubt that the destiny of the Igbo man is firmly rooted to the Igbo-Ukwu culture. Both Igbo-Ukwu culture and Nri culture are so important that writers ought to eschew all forms of narrowness, sentiments and chauvinism in handling them. These remote and immediate cultures help in giving the Igbo man a history.

Uzo Egonu started and ended his analysis on Igbo-Ukwu culture on an impressive note by highlighting the importance of this culture to Africa in particular and to the black race in general. However, either because of inaccurate information or insufficient research, he attempted at re-christening Igbo-Ukwu culture long and widely established as Nri-Igbo-Ukwu culture. He forgot that volumes upon volumes of books have been written on Igbo-Ukwu culture. However, in this work, he recognized the fact that Nigeria Antiquities Department sent Prof. Thurstan Shaw to Igbo-Ukwu to excavate. He also recognized the stack realities that Isaiah Anozie, Richard Anozie and Jonah Anozie (sites) are providentially bona-fide citizens of Igbo-Ukwu. The gentlemen are the owners of the compound upon which the excavations were made from 1959-1964. He is also able to establish the fact that Eze-Nri came from the North through Igala, Aguleri, Agukwu, and Oraeri into Igboland in the late 17th century and early 18th centuries and Eze-Nri made Agukwu his rallying point. It then beats the imagination how he could associate Igbo-Ukwu culture of the 9th century with Nri culture of the 17th century. It is utterly impossible to attempt to tie these two diverse cultures together. No such artifacts were known in Igala, Aguleri, Agukwu or Oraeri. Even more definite is the revelation of the motifs of the artifacts with the artistic forms found in 'sacred' places in Igbo-Ukwu by a team of international archaeologists

Uzo Egonu also represented Igbo-Ukwu as a small village South-West of Onitsha. Here, I would dilate at length a little because this is an area writers on Igbo-Ukwu culture require enough information to aid their future writings and more so, to reverse most of wrong impressions created by some earlier writers on this all important issue.

Igbo-Ukwu, a town in Aguata Local Government Area of Anambra State of Nigeria, is on apex of the highest peak of former Eastern Nigeria, 200 feet above sea level. Its Nkwo market surrounded with ancient myths and legends is almost the greatest purely native market in Igboland. This commands the greatest population in Aguata Local Government Area. Going by the international growth rate of 214 per annum and based on 1963 census figures, Igbo-Ukwu's population is approximated to 55,000 (as at the time of this work). It has three big quarters: Obiuno, Ngo and Ihite. Each of these quarters is a town in itself. In all, there are eleven villages with eleven primary schools and two post primary institutions in Igbo-Ukwu (based on the time of this work, about 1980). Igbo-Ukwu people are very accommodating, religious, peace loving, hardworking. Igbo-

Ukwu is so Igbotic that all the attributes of Igbo people, positive and negative are found per excellence in Igbo-Ukwu persons. This town is until 1942 purely called Igbo. Igbo-Ukwu is surrounded by eleven other burgher towns namely: Azigbo, Amichi, Unubi, Ekwulu-Mili, Ezinifite, Ikenga, Isuofia, Umuona, Agulu-Uzoigbo, Oraeri and Ichida. Two of these towns take their names from Igbo, Azu-Igbo and Agulu-Uzo-Igbo

Among Igbo speaking elements, Igbo-Ukwu has a unique centrality. From Igbo-Ukwu to the last Igbo speaking town in the North, Ihamufu is about equal a distance as from Igbo-Ukwu to the Ndoni, the last Igbo speaking town in the South. From Igbo-Ukwu to Izza, the last Igbo speaking town in the East is about equal a distance as from Igbo-Ukwu to Obialuku, the last Ika Igbo.

Principally, there are two main written dialects in Igbo language: Owerri and Onitsha dialects. Here, many writers on Igbo-Ukwu culture would again require personal contact on this issue to enable them report more accurately and authoritatively. The Igbo language as spoken by an Igbo-Ukwu man whose language has been unadulterated and unaffected by sophistication is actually the culmination of the two dialects. Even the accent and the intonation as uttered by an Igbo-Ukwu man depict the two dialects meeting at a crest. In fact, at Igbo-Ukwu, there is a real amalgamation of both the Owerri and Onitsha dialects of the Igbo language.

All the other nationalities of Nigeria always regard the Igbo man with misgivings, suspicion and mistrust. In fact, the relationship between the Igbo man and every other nationalities of Nigeria borders on hatred. This is due to certain characteristics of the Igbo man. Just as the relationship between the Igbo man and other nationalities border on hatred because of certain characteristics, so is the relationship between an Igbo-Ukwu man and other Igbo speaking elements. The Igbo-Ukwu man is regarded as displaying or representing the original characteristics of the Igbo man in the crudest form. An Igbo-Ukwu was given names like Igbo-Dege, Igbo-Nkwo and so on. Even now, Igbo-Ukwu in some books is styled Igbo-Ukwu Isaiah, Igbo-Ukwu Richard Igbo Umeanadi and so on and these were part of the reasons why the Igbo elites of the past decided to choose their own suffix. These reactions to an unbiased mind should be pregnant with meaning and deserves a down to earth investigation. A thorough on the spot investigation, I am convinced will help writers to call a spade a spade.

The name Igbo-Ukwu is unique in itself. Writers on Igbo-Ukwu culture in handling this area require very sober reflection. Until the late 1930's, the town Igbo-Ukwu had been known and called "Igbo". It was in the early 40's that the suffix "Ukwu" was attached to the name Igbo. No other town had been known and called by this simple name "Igbo". There are other towns with the name Igbo in their names but right from the beginning, these towns had some prefix or suffix originally attached to their names. None of them like Igbo-Ukwu had from origin been sorely and purely called Igbo. Some of the towns are Igbodo, Obi-Igbo, Igbokenyi, Igbosere, Igbo-Eze, Igbo-Etiti, Azigbo, Aguluzoigbo, Igbouzo, Okigbo, Amigbo, Okpalaigbo and so on. It is important to note that all these names are pregnant with meanings. On the faces of all these, I have an ardent belief that the Igbo man does not require a Deus ex machine to help him to develop a studied judicious attitude towards an event that has been very fundamental in giving him a meaningful history.

Coming back to the established fact that Nri culture spread from the North through Igala, Aguleri, Agukwu, Oraeri into Igboland and the fact that Eze Nri made Agukwu his rallying point; I exhort that the importance of this issue is such that great care and caution should be taken in their handling. The Igbo are known as a people imbued with all sorts of discriminations, recrimination and a special tendency of tussling for supremacy. Even where things of much importance to their very existence are concerned, they have never been known to agree. It is high time this typical ugly characteristic of Igbo man to trifle with things significantly precious to him was curbed. The Igbo man would prefer to see that both he and his brother are the losers than live to see his brother alone enjoy a singular glory and recognition. This is more so where things of honour are concerned.

I say this because more than a secret warfare does exist between Oraeri and Agukwu. Both towns tussle for supremacy over Eze-Nri heirloom. A stop ought to be put to this, so that combined effort can be made to project this culture to the outside world. Nri culture and Aro-Chukwu Empire are very precious events in the history helping to give a face-lift to the Igbo. Fighting for supremacy amongst these people does not help in explaining out their historical importance nor does it do the Igbo as a whole any good to juxtapose the 17th century Nri culture against the 9th century Igbo-Ukwu culture.

The archeological remains in Igboland are a true indication of the existence of a rich well organised society under powerful political rulers at the heartland of the Igbo hundreds of years before the coming of the Europeans. The Germans who are the Aryan race claim to be the origin of man on earth. According to the bible, man started life in the Garden of Eden, from which start, later God made the Israelites his chosen people. Historians, on the other hand, hold that man evolved on the African continent, probably in East Africa, some four million years ago. The earliest culture in the world, the Oldowan, evolved in the same place and it was then that man started his bicultural evolutionary development. Over here in Southern Nigeria, many claims exist in myths and legends of powerful significance. The Yoruba talk of Oduduwa, thereby claiming that Ife is the origin of man.

So in Igbo-Ukwu, potent myths and legends exist. There is a firm belief in a group primitively called by their language "Igbo". The popular saying is that in the dim past, "Dake Igbo hie Nkwo". This means that the originators of Igbo were the founders of Nkwo. The saying is more of a canticle than a ballad. The name Igbo is such that it is even today surrounded by mysteries. It is difficult to know whether these Igbo were ordinary human beings a person or a deity having some disciples. In fact, the name is not defined. He is only remembered as coming from the far North in the dim memories. At times, he is allegedly believed to have fallen from the sky. His sacred mission was to found a race and a market, which must help to sustain his large followers because he founded his kingdom on a pinnacle of a summit with gentle slope gradient to the North, South, East and West.

Since he founded his kingdom on a summit not much an arable land, and since he envisaged a large fellowship, he had no alternative than to found the Nkwo market which was more than a human institution for the subsistence of his followers. In actuality, this market really helped to keep his followers together. This saying had it that Igbo had a mysterious broom used once every four days to beckon from far and near all sorts of people to the market even the living and the dead. It is strongly believed today that on Nkwo day, it is very unsafe for one to bend down to look at people going to and coming from the market, otherwise one sees mysterious sights, which may have fatal repercussion on the viewer. Just as in modern Onitsha market, everything from a needle to an anchor can be bought at Nkwo on Nkwo market days. It is also important to note that during the ancient days of inter village wars; there was no fear in going to Nkwo Igbo from distant lands. This "Pax-Nkwoday" needs explaining. Why should the day be a safe day to travel? History always repeats itself. During the last Nigerian civil war, Nkwo market was almost the only source of subsistence to the then Biafra. It is also well in papers that this area is the hardcore of the

Igbo people as seen during the Biafran war. People in this area did not move as other Igbo kingdoms were coming in to take shelter. The Igbo people did not wait for this core to be broken before the eventual submission. This is my sole reason for insisting on the need that writers, especially writers on our history and culture establish personal contact with the inhabitants of the area they write about to enable them obtain a firsthand information of their facts. It is quite unfortunate that Prof. Thurstan Shaw, during his work, could not take down the exact oral traditions existing in the place. It is true that sometimes in the past that people of Igbo-Ukwu had driven Oraeri back in war, but the cause of such wars and the extent of evacuation was never established. The cause was that Avo, the founder of Oraeri was an immigrant who fled from his brothers and found shelter under the protectorate of Igbo. They were settled a faraway off between Adazi-Enu and Igbo-Ukwu and were deriving subsistence from the Nkwo.

It is important to note here that not even the time of the advent of the Oraeri i.e. within 17th century and the time when they were driven back in war i.e. middle 19th century were close to the age of the archeological remains. It is equally important to note that none of the Oraeris' or the present occupants of the land could produce any reliable information about the finds during the Shaw's work. The tradition in Igbo-Ukwu has it that the present occupants of the land were also immigrants from Obiuno into the part of Igbo-Ukwu called Ngo (a village in Igbo-Ukwu). These immigrants as warlords were very instrumental in the conquest of Oraeri, during the time of this said war and so were rewarded by Ngo by being allowed to settle on this part of the land. In actual fact, therefore, it should not beat the imagination why people like Isaiah Anozie and his brothers were ignorant of such deposits.

As we all know, oral tradition alone cannot help Igbo in giving a proper and comprehensive interpretation to the events of their history. Practical application of the knowledge of anthropology is quite inevitable. Anthropologists have dated antiquities of West Africa as follows:

> The Nok culture regarded as the earliest in the West Africa dates from 900 BC to 200 AD. This is followed by Igbo-Ukwu culture of the 9th century. Ife culture comes next starting from the 12th century to the 15th century. Owo culture of the 15th century was followed by Bini culture of the 15th century to the 19th century. Isoede and Esie culture are the latest dating from 16th and the 18th centuries respectively.

From this light, it is completely out of place to compare Igbo-Ukwu culture with Nri culture. Nri culture can only be compared with Bini culture because they belong to the same century. To compare Igbo-Ukwu culture, which is superior to Ife with Nri culture, is indeed out of place. If very serious and consistent research is carried out, Uzo Egonu's probability must rather be found to be the other way round. It might be that Eze Nri fled from the molestation of powerful Northern warlords to find protection under the strong holds that once constituted Igbo sphere of influence.

The mythological founder of the town Igbo-Ukwu, Dege, may not lay any claim to the founding of the Nkwo market. Dege, as it is said had two brothers, Umeadikoba and Idemideku who all settled some distances from the Nkwo and also derived subsistence from the Nkwo. They may or may not have a remote history of migration but they built their dynasty around the Nkwo and as a result were often referred to by other Igbo as "the Igbo people of Nkwo" (Ndi Igbo Nkwo). Perhaps, this regard developed into the people adopting the name Igbo during its amalgamation since the Nkwo was regarded as Nkwo Igbo.

Igbo-Ukwu had never in the past claimed the right of being the religious leader among the Igbo, nor has Igbo-Ukwu any cause to grudge the Aro and Nri the traditional priestly position they occupied in Igboland from the late 19th century. In Igboland, the Nri are the "Levites". The Aro like the Bini had their slaves' empires at the time the British first colonized Eastern Nigeria. Igbo people cannot fail to recognize this. However, Igbo-Ukwu have been from time, a pivot on which all other Igbo communities revolve, the store house of regalia and the royal burial chamber exhumed from the bowels of Igbo-Ukwu soil are artifacts speaking for themselves. It is no mere coincidence; therefore, that Igbo-Ukwu with its position, its culture, its history and its wealth of antiquities had been from origin called Igbo, which is the language group.

Igbo-Ukwu Culture of Agbaenu: The Primordial Igbo Settlement.

The Northern Igbo Culture

The primordial Igbo settlement of Agbaenu mainly lies (as the name suggests) on the escapement at the heartland of the Igbo speaking area. By 'Ndi Agbaenu' we mean a group or a part of the Igbo people that still live along this escapement. This escapement is so called because of its far distance from the sea level (water table). The shallowest valley in this area is well over 200feet above sea level. As a result, there are no flowing waters around this area. The nearest flowing water from the Nkwo which is at the pinnacle of the escapement is over 20km away. Folk memory in this area talks of some valley, which in ancient time held waters. The story of the disappearance or movement of such waters somehow synchronizes with the history of the encroachment of desertification into sub-Saharan Africa, which somehow tells about the age of settlement on this area.

Agbaenu area extends beyond Aguata into Awka in the North, Nnewi and Orlu in the South, Okigwe in the East and parts of Idemili and Aniocha in the West. However, it is wrong to look tenaciously at the Agbaenu concept from the geographical perspective alone. Certain views hold that Agbaenu is not a geographical delineation. The reason being chiefly that the concept is dynamic, widening as the distance of the viewpoint may be. Some for instance will view the Agbaenu as including only those living along Agulu, Ekwuluobia, Amaiyi, Igbo-ukwu up till Nnewi as being the Agbaenu area. Going a little bit further from this area, the whole of Aguata, Aniocha, Nnewi, and times even Orumba and Awka are viewed as being all Agbaenu. On a wider perspective the whole of Anambra State are often taken as being Agbaenu while viewing from other Igbo States. The concept in other words seems to widen geographically or to dilute as we move away from the core. On another hand, some others would classify people as Agbaenu based on characteristic behaviours that are typical about the Igboman and somehow culminated in people from this area. However, experts like professor Afigbo, who canvassed the idea of Nothern Igbo plateau, described this place as the Nri-Awka/Orlu axis, which is more or less a geographical delineation. This area as shown in the map, has Igbo-ukwu at the center of it and Nri, Awka and Orlu at its Northern and Southern frontiers.

At the level of understanding Agbaenu on the basis of characteristic behaviour of the people, the concept seems to acquire some derogatory concept among people that use it, just as it is derogatory to call an Igboman 'Okoro' among other ethnic groups in Nigeria. This derogation also borders on the same reason that breeds contempt and hatred on the Igboman among other ethnic groups in Nigeria. The Agbaenu people believe and prove that they have the archetype of any Igbo tradition or culture and in fact, that they are the prototype of the Igbo man when all the characteristics of the Igboman are put to question. However, it is questionable if they are the only section in Igboland who can make this claim. They believe that their cultural views are more central than any other and so refer to themselves together with some other related areas of Anambra State as the "Igbo-bu-Igbo". There may be need for a critical analysis on the culture of the Agbaenu people to prove this but one fact that is evident is that the Agbaenu people are down to earth in cultural affairs. An on-the-spot investigation should give credence to this. Recent migrations also show that they carry this culture to wherever they migrate. An example of this is the Arondizuogu community, which is an Aro settlement that is principally a collection of populace from Agbaenu and environs. The dialect, culture, thoroughness etc. reveal every element of the Agbaenu people. The centrality of the culture and dialect in this area are not the only aspects that allude to the primacy of this area. The distinctive quality of the Igboman: his business prowess, hardiness, ultra democratic and anti-hegemonic spirit etc. seem to culminate on the people of this are. This is not to say that this tendency is unique with the people of Agbaenu. It is good to note that this distinctive developmental edge may have been because of the population pressure that set in here quite a long time before it did in other areas. The result is that just as the other Nigerians fear and recent the Igboman generally, the rest of the Igbo people recent and fear the Agbaenu man.

Again, the ecological factor of which this area, which originally carried tropical rainforest vegetation had through intense and extended usage been reduced to derived savanna and palm-bush point to the primacy of this settlement. Grotto-chronological evidence in this area shows that the land in the area has been cultivated for nearly six (6) millennia. (Amstrong 1962). In this area, rarely can one come across traditions of movement from any area outside this plateau region. All the communities claim to have moved in or came together from a short distance. On the other hand, most other Igbo groups point to this plateau as the original settlement of their ancestors. As most oral history holds, movement of most Igbo communities appears to have begun from this area.

The reason why the Igbo people first settled on these highlands might quite be an important question. The reason for the dispersion should be another. The population density of this area might quite be an important evidence of ancient occupation. The culmination of the Igbo character on this axis, which attracts great resentment and fear on Agbaenu people from other Igbo, may also form a good line of investigation. However, what I am concerned with putting forward now is that I am dealing with history that underlies every claim and sees a fundamental unity (in spite of all watering) among all the Igbo elements. It is evident that people or the Igbo people settled most anciently in this area but it is arguable the reason why they have gone into Diaspora. It may not be enough to believe a sole religious motive as contained in the work on Igbo-Ukwu culture. I am also very critical of the kind of chauvinism expressed by the presenter of this work as to regard his ambition to present an Igbo-Ukwu culture associated with the town Igbo-Ukwu alone as the Igbo culture. Contrary to this, I will like to widen the view in presenting the Igbo-Ukwu culture as a culture associated with the Agbaenu confederated states.

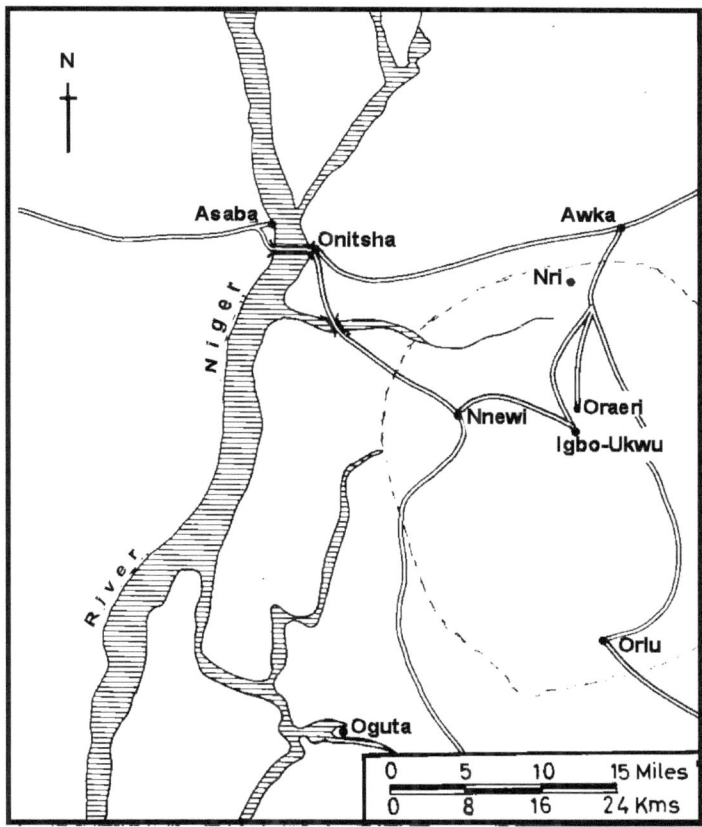

Map showing the Agbaenu area (dotted) with Igbo-Ukwu at the center and Nri, Awka, Orlu, and Onitsha at the outer boarder of this area.

Source: Shaw 1977

Chief in my reasons for this deviation is this; even though the Igbo-Ukwu culture has been proved beyond reasonable doubt to be in the least associable to the Nri culture, why was it impossible for the Igbo-Ukwu people to have an explanation to this culture or even present a least knowledge of its existence. One of the traditions collected by Thurstan Shaw in his first interim report even made an allusion that declared the ownership of the archeological site to belong to Oraeri and not Igbo-Ukwu. (Shaw 1970 P.144). "At a meeting of the Igbo-Ukwu local council in 1964 to discuss a project for a museum, this tradition was challenged and the author taken to task for recording it, as endangering Igbo-Ukwu's claim to the land". " Well of course, everybody knows that the Oraeri people used to be here and that we drove them back in war and that therefore we hold the land by right of conquest" (Shaw; 1970 P.271).

The validity of the above has not been concretized but be it whatever, it may not be of any use to this work since the history of migration and settlement on the area by the Oraeri and history of the conquest and expulsion by the Igbo-Ukwu people are all contemporary history. The debate on who originally owns this land at the time may go on in other works. Here, we are concerned with a history that is far beyond this time and was almost totally lost by then.

Secondly, I have treated in the first part of this work the nature of "states" before the definition of boundaries. I therefore speak of the Agbaenu confederation because prior to the definition of boundaries, lineages or communities were more fragmented, than they exist today. These lineages or groups were independent of each other (as regards rulership) and because of the abundance of land, people could migrate easily anywhere they felt protected or supplied for by nature. People migrated into places far and near and often, are driven by another more powerful or numerous group, a state that may be discussed as anarchic. I have also discussed in detail, the event that brought about the amalgamation of groups into bigger communities to resist wars.

Folk memory is still effective in accounting for such amalgamations. Igbo-Ukwu for instance is one of such towns. Nnewi is another. "Agulu n' Ngiga", a slogan that marked the unification of Agulu, Isuofia is another, Neni, Umuchu whose evolution one author claim to be the inspiration behind Achebe's "Arrow of God". The evidence to this is that almost every primitive community of the Igbo origin especially those around this area are heterogeneous. The various names of the communities have their meaning in the evolution.

Perhaps, Igbo-Ukwu has not been unified by the time they drove Oraeri further since it was only a part of Igbo-Ukwu, Ngo village that drove them far in war. The Ezihu community of Igbo-Ukwu drove Ikenga also a neighbouring town apart. This may also tell something of the sizes of these communities. Perhaps, Igbo-Ukwu was unified during the time of their great war with Nnewi and the like. Like on the international scene, towns like Awka Etiti, Nnobi, Azigbo etc. served as bloc during these wars where also they depend on mercenaries from either of these communities when attacked by any. Okotu brothers have moved from where the Ikenga presently settled in primitive time and later further dispersed into Adazi, Ichida, Amichi etc. they scattered and migrated into other areas before they were forced by event to incorporate their neighbours and form the community as they now exist.

The evolution of the people like the Awka and the people that migrated further like the Dunukofia brother and Amaiyi are well known. People also migrated towards the south, East and West, the evolution of who are simpler depending on the distance of migration and the extent of competition among neighbours. In essence, my effort is to present a picture of events during the time before the beginning of the present shape of things, through which we can see the image of a fundamental culture of the Igbo race, which perhaps, privilege has given its artifacts today to the Igbo-Ukwu people.

If we limit the scope of our vision on dispersion and migration of the Eri and then try to connect this to the rest of the Igbo lineages (an impossible task), how do we account for the disintegration of people in Amaigbo? What do we say of the dispersion and connections among the elements of Amaiyi, Owerri, Okotu, Dunukofia, Ochi, Mbaise, and Okigwe etc? How do we make the assumption on the people that made an early migration into areas like Nsukka-Udi highlands in the North and into Ikwere, Etche, Asa and Ndoki in the South? What about secondary migrations like that of Ngwa from Mbaise? Does the history of the Eri migration and dispersion not synchronize or parallel the growth and dispersion of lineages like:

1. Amaiyi brothers- of Akpo, Umuchu, Achina, Umuomaku, Uga, Nkpologwu, One, Ibugbugu etc. Nkpologwu has a secondary migration of some elements into Nsukka where they maintain a farm settlement and the name Nkpologwu. Umuchu has an element Akukwa that joined Igbo-Ukwu before the amalgamation whereas, Uga has Umueze lineage that built Aguluezechukwu etc.

2. `Umuokotu brothers of Ichida, Adazi-Enu, Adazi-Ani, Adazi-Nnukwu, Obeledu, Amichi, and Osumenyi. Osumenyi further and incorporated other element that kept the community between associating with the Okotu or the Mbanese group in the South. Amichi also incorporated other elements. Ichida like Neni has some element from Eri etc.

3. Mbanese- As the name suggests is a group of five towns that believe that they come from one lineage. They include Ebenato, Utu, Akwaihedi, Ezinifite and Osumenyi.

4. Dunukofia- Ifite Dunu, Ukpo, Umudioka, Umunnachi and Ukwulu. Umudioka elements were also known very primitive to have spread far and wide around the Igboland for their mastery in the Ichi cult. Dioka means the master of Ichi treading and they were invited by people to bring the traditional Ichi that was called Ichi Umudioka. Umudioka are known like the Eri (that brought Ofo culture) to have traveled far spreading the Ichi. We have the Umudioka elements in Awka, Neni, Abagana, Awkuzu etc and all around Imo and Abia state. Umudioka has a wider and primitive spread than the Umueri.

5. Umudiana kindred who are found making the foundation of many communities especially around the Agbaenu or the Northern Igbo plateau. They are found in Adazi-Nnukwu, Neni, Aguleri, Agukwu, etc and are affirmed to be the Adama who provides the Ofo and the Alo to the Nri

6. Umueze kindred are quite another very important element in Igboland, like the Umudiana, virtually forming no homogeneous community but make the founding element of most communities. Umueze are found in Uga. The Umueze also founded Aguluezechukwu. A very important element in Igbo-Ukwu, Isuofia, Neni, Agulu etc. In fact, Umueze are in more than 1/3 the communities in Igboland and they are often the most primitive or principal settlers wherever they are found. Umueze are also the element that built the Igbo-Uzo (Ibuzo) across the Niger and many communities in Enugu-Udi area and on the Orlu axis. We have the Umueze-Ka-Mmadu the most primitive element in Agukwu (Nri) and Umuezeora kindred formed the foundation of Aguleri the most primitive settlement of Eri

7. Umuezechima- An important lineage that is among the elements that crossed the Niger. The communities include:
    -   Obomkpa, Onicha-Ukwu, Onicha-Ugbo, Obor,

IsseleUkwu, Issele Asagba, Issele Mkpitime, Onicha Oloma, Onitsha, Ezi, Ogwashi Ukwu. From every analysis, these elements prove to be Igbo but some events of history and perhaps, the aberrations associated with modern Igbo historians, make them allude to Benin origin. Significantly, Onicha is not only found in this area of the Igbo culture but also in Nsukka and even in the Imo state suggesting a dispersion of culture from a point. It was not only Umuezechima who fall under the lineage that crossed the Niger. Some others did and also faced the retrace after the encounter with Benin. Oko for instance have the parent community across the Niger, like wise Akwa-Ukwu. It should equally be treasured in the mind that this Umuezechima might have something to do with the Umueze lineage.

8. Ochi- Basically few but another powerful theocracy in the Igbo-culture. Made up of Nnewi, Oraifite and Ochi and had their theocracy built around the "Edo". At times, generally referred to as Anaedo. The elements are also found in many other communities where there are as much as fragments that are completely drowned into the community.

9. Mbaise is another powerful theocracy in the South, with very large lineages, which got amalgamated in the event of their history. Ezinifite, Ahiara, Ekwerazu, Oke-Ovuvu, Agabaja, Mbutu etc. The Ngwa community also trace their origin back to this theocracy likewise many other separate communities in this area.

10. Amaigbo- Near Orlu is the father of a multitude of communities scattered around the Orlu axis and even further to the South.

11. Many other lineages exist with such connections that could be paralleled with the Eri or the Aro lineages, but the much mentioned already should throw enough light on the picture. Again, a philological study of some communities, though they may be rivals, prove them to be similar or same origin e.g. the Ikwo, Izzi and Ezza on the North eastern part of Igboland. Igbo-Ukwu elements, Ezinifite, Ekwulummili, Ekwulobia, Ikenga, Azigbo etc from evidence from philology also prove to be primitively similar.

On the other hand, the theocratic hegemony of the Nri may be paralleled with the Aro mercantilism or the Awka smithing network and the Umudioka artistic expertise.

1. Eri had their element settled in Agulu-Eri, Enugwu-Agidi, Agukwu, Ozu, Oraeri, Igbariam, Amanuke, Umuleri, Nando, and Awkuzu. There are also some elements as parts of communities like Enugwu-Ukwu, Neni, Nawfia, Akamkpisi, Nnokwa, Ogbunike, Ichida, and Amesi and in far away Idah. Their theocratic hegemony also went beyond those towns into some foreign elements.

2. Aro- had their principal elements settled in Aro-Oke-Igbo (Arochukwu) and Aro-Ama-Nkwu that founded the Aro-Ndizuogu. They have their other elements in places like Ndiowu, Ajalli, Ndikelionwu, and Ndiokpalaeze. They have most parts scattered everywhere as parts of communities especially around the Orlu axis. There is an Aro element forming a village in Ihiala, Aro as part of Mbutu section of Mbaise etc. The theocracy around the Ibini Ukpabi and the Aro mercantilism was even more pronounced and far-reaching than the Eri.

3. Umudioka- Umudioka is a part of Dunukofia with their brothers settled as Ifitedunu, Ukpo, Umunnachi and

Ukwulu. They mastered the Ichi or tattooing cult and spread it around the Igboland. They had several settlements in Imo and Abia state where they still retain the same name (Umudioka). They are also found as part of communities like Neni, Abagana, and Awkuzu etc.

4. Awka- Awka established her theocracy around the Agbala-Oracle but what gave it ascendancy is the smiting culture. Its oracle network was not as developed as the Aro network but with the merchanting of the smith culture, they were able to travel around parts of Igboland though strictly guarding the knowledge of the culture from other people. The smiting culture was not restricted to Awka but was found in many other communities in small scales or in large scales like in Abriba and Nkwerre.

This is just to mention a few of the Igbo lineages. There are many more and even large ones. The question now becomes, how would the Igbo history of origin look like if each of these lineages in their schismatic spirit trace the Igbo history on their lineage? Or, if each would establish an origin at the point where they could not trace the descent any further? Reason should carry us beyond these secondary developments in the society.

What would one have to say about names of communities that have the name Igbo attached to them? Certainly, the Igbo do not give a name without meaning or reason. For instance, we see Igbo-eze (which means the kingly Igbo), Igbo-Etiti (Igbo dwelling at the center), Igbo-Uzo now Ibusa (on the way Igbo), Igbokenyi (Igbo is greater than the elephant), Igbodo etc. What could one have to say about these communities that are scattered around everywhere in Igbo areas? What about Amaigbo, (the shore of the Igbo), which historically we know some Igbo elements to have dispersed from this point. Again take a look at Igbo-Ukwu, primitively called "Igbo" and towns settled around it like Azigbo (the back of the Igbo), a small town just immediately after Igbo-Ukwu, Aguluuzoigbo, (the way between Agulu and Igbo), another small town settling between Agulu and Igbo-Ukwu etc. The meanings in such names as Amaigbo (the shore of the Igbo), Obigbo (the heart of Igbo) or Aro-Oke-Igbo (The Aro of the great Igbo), Okpalaigbo (the first son of the Igbo) etc ought to be thoroughly investigated.

Surprisingly however, none of these communities scattered to the East, West, North and South and with Igbo-Ukwu at the center make any claim to the Igbo culture. Even with the determined meanings in the names. On the other hand, it is the Eri occupying a section of the Northern part of the Igbo and which has nothing in connection with the Igbo culture in their traditional names that makes this claim. Eri talks of Nri, Umuleri, Aguleri, and Oraeri etc all but Eri and nothing Igbo. The Igbo culture must be something else, something deeper and wider than Eri.

The pattern of settlement by communities after a breakup or fusion of communities is often embedded in the names they take-like the Onicha-Ugbo, Onicha-Ukwu, and Onicha-Olona, the names taken by Azuigbo and Agulu-Uzoigbo around Igbo-Ukwu. The neighboring towns like Ekwulumili, Ezinifite and Ekwuluobia might reveal things about their early migration and settlement from their names. Ezinifite for instance, has a village, which goes by the name Amaekwulu meaning the shores of the Ekwulu, and just after that village is the town Ekwulumili, itself previously known as Ekwulu or Ekwuluatulu meaning "Ekwulu abounds". Yet on the other side of Ezinifite is another settlement that goes by the name Ekwuluobia meaning the "Ekwulu who are visitors"? The philology of these towns also gave them a primitive linkage. Another of such town is Amaobia (meaning the shore of visitors), a small town near Awka, which have their history of acceptance and settlement as a collection of immigrants from different places including Aro. They were from origin known as foreigners and called by the name.

Surely, a great deal of anthropological work still need to be done on the Igbo cultural origin and such work must have to take a liberal perspective. Perhaps, the account on an Igbo theocracy built around the Nkwo may be correct. It was sometime disclosed of a wall that enclosed a large area in the past. A wall that enclosed parts of Igbo-Ukwu, Azigbo, Awka-Etiti, Amichi and Ogbodu near Ekwulumili. The remains of this wall could still be seen today. Set aside, the idea of the Igbo-Ukwu people themselves and take a look at the Nkwo, which was anciently built on the apex of the Igbo heartland. The Nkwo was in ancient times called Nkwo Igbo and not Nkwo Igbo-Ukwu. The people living around here were primitively called Ndi-Igbo Nkwo. Even in this modern era, the common parlance from people going to trade in Nkwo is "let us go to Nkwo Igbo". People come from every nook and cranny, far and near, of the Igbo land to trade in this market. Take also a look at the trend of settlements around the Nkwo perhaps for subsistence. Look at the pattern of migration of the Eri, from the Northern origin at Aguleri, down towards the Nkwo, up to Nri and Oraeri. The pattern of migration of the Aro towards this center might also have some important implication, likewise that of Awka. The pattern of the movement of the entire Igbo during the Biafran war towards the core may all sum together to prove this point to be the core of the Igbo culture or simply the Rome of ancient Igbo civilization. Of course, the Igbo will not wait for this core to be broken before their final surrender in the war.

Perhaps, the Igbo-Ukwu people cannot make a claim on this market, which dominate their name. Other Igbo only regard them in ancient times as "Ndi-Igbo Nkwo" and perhaps providence had given them this creation. It was during the amalgamation of the towns that make up the Igbo-Ukwu town that the people officially took that name "Igbo" and had "Ukwu" added to it in early 40's to differentiate it from the language tribe. The building of the Nkwo market on the pinnacle of Igboland might have a great deal to tell about the people who settle here (on the high lands).

Communities around the Agbaenu and all the highly competitive areas are mainly heterogeneous communities comprising various elements. It is rare to find around this areas, communities that are homogenous. This is simply because of the social events that brought a revolution upon the traditional social order that I have already detailed on. Stronger groups pushed people from place to place and people migrated easily because of population pressure or for the purpose of Agriculture. The social changes, population pressure and lately, the Aro adventure forced many communities in spite of their general differences to merge.

The Neni community, a town in Aniocha Local Government Area of Anambra State, paints a good picture of such communities thereby formed. Neni town partly comprise of UMUDIOKA, a village which has every element of Umudioka in Dunukofia Local Government Area and still has the evidence of coming from this place; UMUEZE, another distinctive part of Neni that trace their origin to the Umueze of Uga in Aguata Local Government Area; AMAKWA, another part of Neni that trace their origin to the Amakwa of Ozubulu in Ekwusigo Local Government Area; UMUNRI, that trace their source to be Eri, a culture whose spread I have elaborately discussed. There are also other elements in Neni that claim different origins and those that claim aboriginal status. Most other communities along the Agbaenu axis and beyond are similarly composed. Communities that migrated earlier but had to assimilate other immigrants to increase their numbers for social security also reflect the same structure.

It may be quite important to look at the nature of naming of the section in such heterogeneous communities so formed. They are not usually partitioned on the genial basis because of the heterogeneity. Usually, we find divisions like

- Ikenga and Ifite (Ihite and Ikenga)
- Ezi and Ifite (Ezi na Ifite)
- Obi n' Uno (Obiuno) and Obi n' agu (Obeagu) or Obin'ugbo, Obi n' etiti (Etiti) and Obi n' eziagu (Ezagu)
- Iruowelle and Eziowelle (Owelle)
- Obi n' ngo (Ngo) or Ndi enugwu (Enugwu) and Ndi Agbo or Ndi ani mmiri (Mba Mmiri)
- Obi n' Owelle and Obi n' Aba or Nkwelle...?
- Iruigbo, Azuigbo, Ezigbo, Uzoigbo, Abigbo, Anigbo etc

Communities or elements that are more homogenous are often identified by "Umu" prefix to the name of the progenitor. These characterize the nature of village division among many heterogeneous communities and in some cases identify autonomous communities by virtue of their location in relation to other communities. All these realities need a down to earth and unbiased investigation before a quick conclusion is drawn on them.

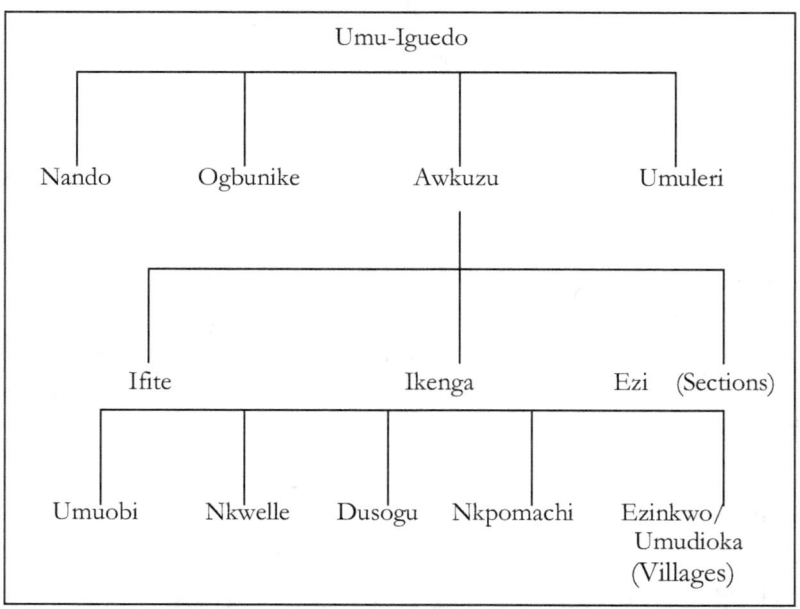

Take for instance; Oguejiofor J.O made an illustration of the villages, sections and lineages in Awkuzu, which he claimed to be a homogenous community and descendant of Iguedo, the daughter of Eri. (Oguejiofor J.O; 1996 P.31): " This Iguedo (who is a woman) had four sons who were the fathers of Ogbunike, Nando, Awkuzu and Umuleri. Awkuzu had three sons who begot Ifite, Ezi and Ikenga of which he analyzed the descendants of Ikenga on a genial tree as thus illustrated above:

Considering the status of such a scholarly work, one is left in the cold when wondering if Ifite, Ikenga and Ezi were really personal names. Certainly, Ifite, Ikenga and Ezi were no real names and it beats the imagination why such a research could not trace the real names of the descendants at this level whereas, it could go beyond that to trace the name of Awkuzu their father and even the mother of Awkuzu, Iguedo. This raises a more fundamental question about the claims of Eri culture and all its adherents. Again, among the villages that make up Ikenga section, we find elements like Nkwelle, Ukpomachi, and even Umudioka. In the analysis we also see Umudunu as one of the lineages descending from Dusogu. Such lineages simply raise suspicion about early linkage with the elements of other cultures especially their neighbors - the Dunukofia. Are these elements not simply an amalgamation of different and some related immigrant that are divided into the section under a name Awkuzu? Is their affiliation to Eri not only as a result of factors that I have earlier discussed or perhaps as a result of direct influence from Eri culture towards its amalgamation or unification? Or would this culture be wholly and simply viewed through an Eri spectacle? Above all, when did the Igbo start tracing decent from female line. If Iguedo was a woman who married among the pre-existing Igbo communities, why should this lineage be matrilineal? This exposes how verbose the claim of communities linking themselves to the Eri. Likewise are many other communities that lay such claims such as Enugwu-Ukwu, Nawfia etc.

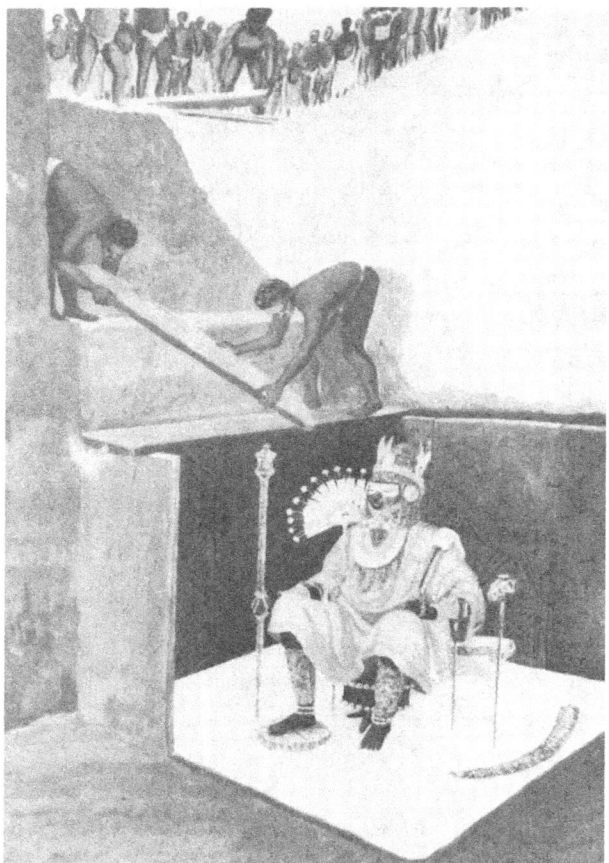

The assumed structure of Burial Kings in Igbo-Ukwu culture.

Source: Shaw 1977

PART II

Chapter Three

The Importance of Archeology to the History of the Igbo

I have somewhere in the early pages of this work distinguished between history, which means the whole corpus of knowledge of the past of man, and history, which means the written records of the past. The history of the Igbo has to depend as far as the nation itself is concerned on every kind of evidence other than history, since for the greater part of the time she Igbo race is assumed to be a race without history worthy of speaking of, prior to the second half of the 19th century. Igbo race has no written traditions. Oral tradition may not be elaborate especially when it has passed through a long period of time.

Again, judging from the proud nature of Igbo, which renders everyone into trying to prove himself as a progenitor of the whole tribe, every folk account therefore becomes suspect. It becomes necessary that one begin to look elsewhere for more scientific and reliable proofs and most likely axiomatic judgments. To this point therefore, archeology and such related disciplines should be of greater importance to the history of Igbo. African history is quite unlike the history of Europe and America where there have long existed the written traditions and other reliable methods. This is not to rule out the role of archeology entirely from such history since some additional evidence of the material culture, manner and customs is being revealed by this science. As I mentioned in this work, it must not be forgotten that the further we go back in history, the thinner the record becomes and not unnaturally the early historians, painfully copying by hand all the records of wars, dynasties, religious persecutions or conversions, migrations and revolutions, should not afford time for description of the chamber pot of the time. This is simply because of the absence of any printing press at the time or any safer method of duplication.

One of the ways in which archeology can be of particular use to this study may be to date cultural materials from at least a little way in land, whose horizon is unknown by iron of imported wares. With the discovery of carbon dating, it is now possible to insert a series of sequence of some probable dates from which a whole series can be placed in reasonable chronological order.

In the proceeding of events, even though we treasure the possibility in mind, we should avoid any tendency of thinking the Igbo as once being center of a great civilization. On such assumption, we would be making a false hypothesis, though such artifacts got from archeology can rather act as a basis of a culture. We should expect to find the cultural artifact in little things like the tomb of a titled man or king. We may not expect to find so much like the great pyramids of Egypt or the tomb of a Pharaoh. Let us not start off on a false basis, which can only lead to disappointment and disgust. It is not necessary for us at this stage to continue hovering aimlessly on chaotic doggerel. Let us look at thing as they are and not as we want them to be or think them to be. Luckily, we now have the disclosure of the archeological finds in Igbo-Ukwu, which has been excavated by Professor Thurstan Shaw. Several events have also taken part in the history of Africa, which we know little or much about. The natural occurrence of materials and human ingenuity in the past we also know something about. Let us see if such can be any use to our research.

The Archeological Finds in Igbo-Ukwu

The Igboman used to be regarded as without a history. The Yoruba had until the recent discoveries and archeological excavations made by Prof. Thurstan Shaw at Igbo-Ukwu felt that they were the only race in Southern Nigeria with a history. This feeling was based on Ife arts and cultures, which were in vogue at the time the Europeans, first set their feet on Nigerian soil. Recent development in Igbo-Ukwu has proved this assertion null and void. It now has been proved that as the Yoruba and Bini arts and culture were flourishing during the advent of the Western civilization, because the Onis and Obas were still holding their sway as powerful rulers, the great rulers in Igboland were in their wane. Empires rise and fall. This does not mean to assert that there has been some great civilization in the area, which has fallen, but the research and excavations made in Igbo-Ukwu have proved the existence of some great culture and society in antiquity.

Archeological finds in Igbo-Ukwu give proof to the fact that the Igboman has immense history. These finds, according to archeologists and anthropologists date earlier than Yoruba arts and culture. Antiquities of West Africa have been dated as follows:

> The Nok culture regarded as the earliest in West Africa dates from 900BC to 200AD. This is followed by Igbo-Ukwu culture of the 9th century. Ife culture comes next starting from the 12th century to the 15th century. Owo culture of the 15th century was followed by Bini culture starting from the 15th to 19th century. Tsoede and Esie cultures are the latest dating from the 16th to the 18th centuries respectively.

The archeological remains in Igbo-Ukwu are a true indication of the existence of a rich well organised society under powerful political rulers at the heart of Igboland hundreds of years before the coming of the Europeans. Germans who are the Aryan race claim to be the origin of man on earth, while according to the Bible, man started life in the Garden of Eden from which start later, God made the Israelites, His chosen people. Historians and anthropologists on the other hand hold that man evolved on the African continent probably in East Africa, some four million years ago. The earliest culture in the world, in Oldowan, evolved in the same place and it was then that man began his bicultural evolutionary development (handy man). Coming down to

Southern Nigeria, the Yoruba talk of Oduduwa, thereby claiming that Ife is the origin of man. This assertion is supported by the Ife arts and culture but this is not to say that this claim is factual. Coming home a little further, the Nri culture claims that Eri came down from heaven and settled at Awka, with some artifacts to show. However, they do not make claims of being the origin of the Igbo but that of Eri children alone. The finds in Igbo-Ukwu, which date many hundreds of years earlier than Ife arts and Eri culture should have shaken the Yoruba and to a greater intensity, the Nri. These finds in Igbo-Ukwu must as a fact bring a complete transformation in Igbo, West Africa and African history.

Many possess very scanty knowledge about the archeological finds in Igbo-Ukwu and very few, especially in this modern era, have come in contact with the work of Prof. Thurstan Shaw on these finds. For this reason, therefore, I would wish to make a little summary of the works, speculations and conclusions of Shaw rather than mention this archeological finds only in passing as most authors do.

Review of Thurstan Shaw's "Unearthing Igbo-Ukwu"

The very stroke that sparked off this research was the discoveries made by Isaiah Anozie during the 12th month, before the outbreak of the Second World War in 1939, when he was digging a cistern. The cistern is the traditional way of preserving surface water for use during the dry season because of the water difficulties experienced by people in this area during dry season. Such cisterns are getting phased out because of the advent of pipe-borne water supply. Mr. Isaiah discovered quite a number of items when he was digging the cistern. Ignorant enough, he only used them in decorating his sitting room and sold the rest to his neighbours and people who felt it could be potent for making charms. It was through the help of the District Officer who was enlightened enough and who realized the importance of such artifacts, when he became aware of them that the Department of Antiquities came to the knowledge of it.

"At this point in time, the town which the discoveries were made was referred to as 'Igbo' and this is the name marked on most maps. It was later that the suffix 'Ukwu' was added to it, i.e. Igbo-Ukwu meaning 'Great Igbo' - to distinguish from other places called 'Igbo'. The name Igbo-Ukwu became increasingly necessary, since linguists are using the same spelling 'Igbo' for the name of the people who live in this part of Nigeria and for the language they speak. No other town had been known and called by this name 'Igbo'. There are towns with the word in their name but right from the onset, these towns had some prefix or suffix originally attached to their names. None of them like Igbo-Ukwu had from origin been solely and purely called Igbo.

Professor Thurstan Shaw was invited from London to carry out this archeological work in 1958 and he arrived Nigeria in November 1959. After a number of visits to the cultural centers in Nigeria and contacts with relevant individuals, he arrived Igbo-Ukwu and made the necessary negotiations that would make him free to work. When everything was ready, he made excavation at three different locations in Isaiah Anozie, Richard Anozie and Jonah Anozie's compound though not all at the same time. These men are notably, indigenes of Igbo-Ukwu.

The result of the excavation was a very mighty revelation. The result of the first digging in 1960 in Isaiah's compound interpreted to be 'a store house for regalia' revealed over 50 different items made of bronze, brass, copper, iron, clay, ores and several heaps of beads. They were significantly made with very highly experienced artistic acumen. Among the items disclosed were:

1. Bronze roped pot
2. Bronze alter stand
3. Heap of Iron knives

4. Globular pot with stopper
5. Copper spiral snake ornament
6. Collapsed globular pot with stopper
7. Pottery overlying bronze bowl
8. Smaller bronze bowl
9. Longer bronze bowl
10. Plagues of composite belt
11. Mass of copper wire
12. Pedestal pot on its side
13. Mass of beads
14. Rows of beads
15. Beads
16. Iron-sword blade in two piece
17. Copper scabbard-support
18. Bronze pendant ornament (elephant head)
19. Associated rows of beads
20. Associated crotals
21. Copper ring
22. Spiral-headed copper staples
23. Bronze crotals
24. Rows of fine spiral copper bases
25. Bronze pendants ornament (double egg)
26. Beads and Copper wire attached to the pendant ornament
27. Semicircular copper handle for calabash
28. Semicircular copper handle for calabash
29. Bronze shell
30. Copper handle for calabash
31. Bronze staff head
32. Iron blade associated with staff head
33. Iron objects
34. Iron objects probably calabash fittings
35. Ring of dark substance inside rings.
36. Three copper ring
37. Copper handle for calabash

38. Pieces of Calabash
39. Decorated pieces of calabash with copper handle attached
40. Part of copper handle for calabashes
41. Human molar tooth
42. Pieces of cloth
43. Pieces of Bronze chain
44. Broken lower end of Bronze sword scabbard
45. Copper handle for calabash
46. Four bronze canine teeth.

The list excludes the number of items already dug out by Isaiah himself while digging a cistern. Though some of these items were sold, some have been recovered among which is a bronze pendant ornament in form of a leopard's head etc.

The digging in the compound of Mr. Richard Anozie the same year was understood to be a burial chamber of a titled man or a priest king. Among the disclosure made from this chamber were many different items, which include:

1. Northern most elephant tusk
2. Decorated copper roundels
3. Crown
4. D-Shaped decorated copper plate
5. Pectoral plate
6. Copper bracket
7. Copper anklet
8. Copper Strap
9. Skull
10. Pair of Copper anklets
11. Circle of spiral copper bosses set in wood
12. Copper and bead anklets
13. Another part of copper
14. Copper handle for a calabash
15. Middle elephant tusk

16. Tangled copper fan-holder
17. Group of six copper anklets
18. Group of three copper anklets
19. Another copper bracket
20. Copper staff supporting the bronze leopards skull
21. Bronze horseman hilt
22. Southern most elephant tusk and many pieces of iron.

The final digging that was carried out in 1964 at Mr. Jonah Anozie's compound revealed yet more items. The report of Jonah prior to the excavation was that things had been found on this site when clay for compound walls had been dug out. It was said that a large quantity of beads were found and some bronze objects among which there was a table; though some of these items were never recovered again. The digging exposed the place to be a repository.

Among the items revealed at this spot were:
1. 15 copper or bronze wristlets
2. Four heavier copper wire
3. Copper rod, some 15cm long
4. Iron funnel
5. Small bronze bell
6. Large crotal with two chain links attached
7. Broken top of another small decorated bell
8. Two cylindrical staff ornament
9. Paper thin casting of a similar cylindrical ornament
10. Two copper bars with expanded ends
11. Lots of pottery etc.

According to Thurstan Shaw, one interesting thing about the bronzes found at Igbo-Ukwu was that their style and their decoration were quite unlike the well-known bronzes of Benin and Ife. It shows the exclusivity of the cultures from each other and for the difference in age (time). There was no way a comparison could be made among the three. The finds at Igbo-Ukwu being also scientifically and artistically superior demands a new different channel of inquiry.

From analysis of the items from the digging, it is clear that the bronze pot had been made in the pattern of most of the Agbaenu pieces still in use in the area, "Ite-otu". They were also made in the method of Benin and Ife bronzes i.e. by the lost wax method. The principle of this method is simple, although its execution can be very complex and call for a great deal of skill. The principle is to make a model of wax and then replace it with bronze. This is because wax can be easily modeled into any desired shape. The procedure goes from modeling wax into any shape and removed over fire through a hole. When bronze is heated sufficiently, it becomes molten and can be poured into the mould through a hole, where it will set hard in the shape of the mould. The clay is then removed.

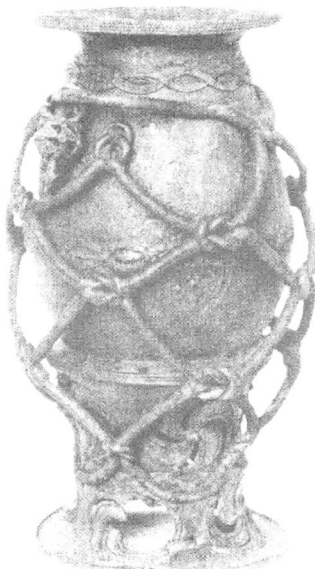

The Bronze Roped Pot
Source: Shaw 1977

The procedure is used for casting solid objects such as the belt plague which is found in Isaiah's compound. However, for the making of larger objects, a clay core has to be used in order to save wasting metal by making the casting hollow, and this makes the procedure more complicated. The core of clay is modeled roughly to the shape of the inside of the desired object, and mounted on a clay pedestal or base. The core is then covered with a large layer of wax, which now receives the details of shape and pattern ultimately desired for the bronze object. The whole mould is covered with clay and wax melted off through pouring duct created by adding a rod of wax. The bronze is melted and poured into the mould through the pouring duct and allowed to set.

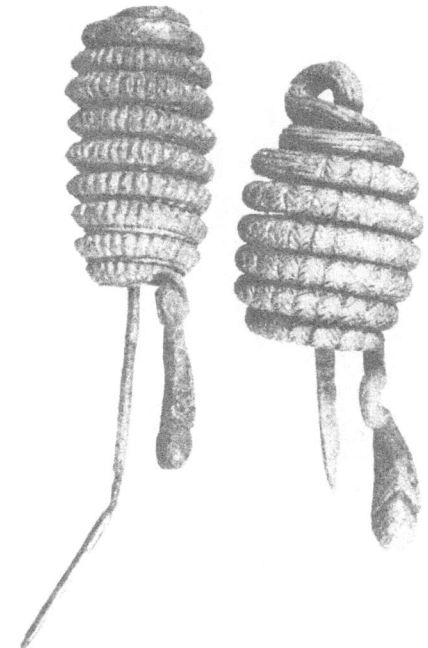

The Copper Spiral bonze Ornament
Source: Shaw 1977

These procedures reveal the complexity in such molding, which is described elaborately by Thurstan Shaw in his work: Unearthing Igbo-Ukwu. From this description as well, it is realized that in the lost wax method, each can only be used once resulting in the uniqueness of each casting. The complexity of the designs and pattern used in decorating these items were immense and unique in character and over 63,200 beads were found in Isaiah's compound, many of them lying in rows. Among the findings were also spiral snake ornaments which consist of a square sectioned spike of copper running through a spirally coiled length copper and which terminate in the snake's head, holding an egg in its mouth. These decorations were not made by being molded in wax before casting, but were achieved with a sharp-ended punch hammered into cold metal. It is remarkable that analysis has shown that objects from Igbo-Ukwu made in this fashion are composed of almost pure copper, while the objects made by the wax casting process are composed of bronze. What is interesting about this is the indication it gives to us of the metallurgical knowledge of the craftsmen who made the metal objects of Igbo-Ukwu. Copper can be bent, twisted, inscribed and have designs punched into it in a cold state much more easily than bronze, while bronze flows more easily when molten and is better for casting than copper.

There were a number of fascinating and interesting items found in the digging. Thanks to the expertise of Shaw who splinted his hairs in interpreting and fitting the broken items together to obtain the true pictures. Among the items he discovered the staff ornaments, which were among the most complex and most highly decorated of all Igbo-Ukwu casting (details in Shaw's work "Unearthing Igbo-Ukwu). In his attempt to situate some of these items in history, he discovered the bronze casting of shell, which was assumed to be in imitation of the giant Africa land snail (Achatina).

However, no less than four different experts on shells to whom photographs have been shown concur in the opinion that it is a triton shell (Charoina), which is represented in each case. The coast where such shells occur is only 180kilometer (100 miles) away, but the identification of the form of these bronze vessels with that of a seashell may well have important implications.

The two human head ornaments are among the most attractive casting from the digging. They bear the same pattern of facial scarifications radiating in four directions from the bridge of the nose, which are the same pattern with the human heads decorating one of the cylindrical staff ornament. This is clearly in resonance with the age long and dying practice in the area called "Ichi" - A number of animal heads such as the leopard head, snakes, snail, elephant tusk etc form little or no basis for speculations on the nationality of these items.

> Had the remain been as recent as only a hundred years ago, it is almost certain that amongst them we should have found something which could be recognized as import of Europe. However, we found nothing of this kind. Some of the glass beads and some of the rusted iron object might have been imports from Europe, but they were not recognizable and unequivocally so. If the remains belonged to any time during the last 450 years, there was always the possibility of finding a European import and had we done so, it could have been possible to say that the associated find could not have been older than the date of that import.

This created some difficulty in dating the finds and there was no other obvious relevant clue to dating the finds. Shaw was therefore limited to using carbon dating and he was very careful in preserving specimens of charcoal found in the deposits. Again, there were lots of ambient to the find in Isaiah's compound. It proved difficult initially to analyze the routine of such deposits, but after series of severe studies, Shaw was able to say that:

> "I came to the conclusion that what was found in Isaiah's compound was neither a burial nor a pit hurriedly dug to receive hidden treasures. Yet, treasure it undoubtedly was, in one sense, in that the bronzes and beads must have represented a considerable

concentration of wealth in society not enjoying a money economy....

The most likely interpretation seems to be that the deposit represents a store of such regalia and ceremonial objects, carefully placed and preserved, but for some reason abandoned. Ceremonial objects are sometimes intentionally buried between the occasion of their ritual use, and I wondered if Isaiah's digging had stumbled upon an instance of this practice. However, this did not seem likely in view of the way in which the objects appear to be laid out in a rectangular area all more or less on one level and at no great depth. If a pit is dug to hide things, at a time of emergency or for safe keeping between ceremonies, it is likely to be deeper, and less extensive in area, and to have things piled in one on top of the other. The only definite super position in the deposit appeared to be that of a decorated calabash found over the pendant double egg ornament and its attached chains; the staff head overlying the bronze shell, looked as if it might have fallen there. Such a shrine for keeping sacred vessels and regalia between the occasions of their use is likely to have been protected by light walls on two or three sides and by roofing. It is possible that the collapse of a pole from such a roof was responsible for the crushing of one of the pair of globular pots and not the weight of the wall which was built on top of it...After the abandonment and the collapse of any structure, vegetation would have quickly covered the site and all memory of it was apparently lost.

These were the speculations and interpretations credited to Thurstan Shaw on the findings. Unfortunately, during the time of this research, the priest kings in Igboland were already in their wane, Shaw, in search of clues to difficulties created by these finds, turned to a nearby small town called Oraeri which was still on a younger level of social metamorphosis, because it still had some relic of a past king. Though Shaw, innocent enough was only seeking to give explanations to why the hut and its content should have been abandoned intact and as to how come the content of the burial chamber at Richard Anozie's compound. Shaw also treasured in his speculations that the likely reasons may be that the place was overrun in warfare or slave raiding and the sacred store house was either missed by the invading party or else left alone as being too dangerous to tamper with, since it was clearly the repository of other men's' deities. This speculation was particularly stimulated by the fact that in his collection of past wars, he collected that Oraeri was once driven back by Igbo-Ukwu in war. But unfortunately, Shaw could not spare time to find out the exact area, which Oraeri was driven back from. Again, he did not care much about the time of this war and the cause. How can the war be very much in mind whereas the wounds were forgotten? It is not likely in any way that Oraeri knew anything about the deposit or else, the war being not too long ago, would have not got such a great culture easily over run. A great layer of soil could not have covered an area abandoned just in the 19th century when the said war took place. Shaw, being actually moved by such records, went to find out from Oraeri what was there, hoping to find facts on which to build on. Shaw was disappointed at the findings he made at Oraeri having found the few regalia there at his disposal to be very modern wares and imported, without any trace of relation with the findings at Igbo-Ukwu.

> I was told that among the Eze's regalia was a special cup, which was so sacred that I could not be shown it on that occasion, if I wished to see it, I would have to come back again some days later, after having presented a sheep for the necessary sacrifice. Imagining that this sacred cup might be a bronze vessel, I reckoned that it would be worth the price of a sheep to see it, and if possible, photograph it. After presenting the sheep, I returned some days later and waited with some excitement for the sacred cup to be brought forth. When it finally appeared, it proved to be a China Toby jug.

This goes a long way into exposing the inferiority of such a culture. The oral traditions collected by Shaw, are very much distorted. Since neither the previous inhabitants, nor the present inhabitants had any knowledge of such deposit nor could produce any explanation to it because of their ignorance. Hence, Thurstan Shaw did not actually bring his work to a completion. He couldn't have gone any further than we ourselves who are the Igbo could go. It is time then for all to keep aside the struggle as to which the culture belongs and think of the cultural implications on those finds which abound. Traces of the cultures dumped in the soils of Igbo-Ukwu are not only found in Igbo-Ukwu or Oraeri today but all over the Igboland and even the world over. The question now is how to put these symbols and cultures together to build our history.

Take for instance, the copper spiral snake ornament that is driven into the end of a wooden staff. This is seen in the Jewish culture when Moses made the fiery serpent (made of bronze) and mounted it on a wood that, whoever is bitten by a serpent and looked unto it, shall not die (Number 21:4-9). This symbol has remained the symbol of medicine and of life till date as seen in emblems of medical doctors. This is known as the ancient culture of Hippocrates (460-377BC) the Greek physician who founded on the Aegean Island of Cos, a school of Medicine that laid the foundation of Clinical Medicine and is recognized by common consent as the father of medicine. Medical doctors up till date, take the Hippocratic oath before they are vested with authority. The pot found with some dead dry leaves inside it confirms also the medical tenets of some of these finds. It is not a coincidence that the snake is having an egg in its mouth also pointing towards life.

One of the snail shells was seen with a cross on the base, which significantly might have some implications. Most of the other objects are decorated with coiled snakes which occurrence is parallel to a culture in the area of the taboo against killing and eating the python. Significantly again, one of the items is a bronze horseman hilt, which came from the burial chamber. It beats the imagination therefore, how this could come about since there was no presence of such animals in the area until about 1000AD, when such animals, were brought by the Arabs to Northern Nigeria. How come the knowledge of such motif then? If these things were of imported ideas, from where could they be? All these must come together to help us trace the aborigines of the Igbo man and not think that God threw Eri down from heaven and people were created at Orlu, Owerri and Mbaise and all eventually came together to become one and formed a new culture called Igbo culture.

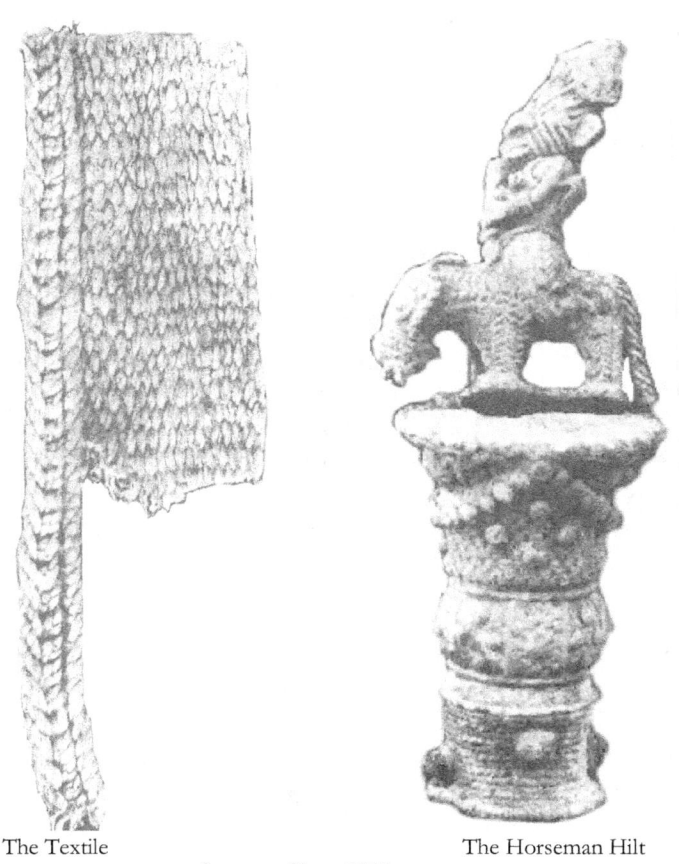

<table>
<tr><td>The Textile</td><td>The Horseman Hilt</td></tr>
</table>

Source – Shaw 1977

I wish to pre-empt here that a lot more are still left undisclosed in the bowels of Igbo-Ukwu. Beads and items have been found in different locations in Igbo-Ukwu especially around the part of Ngo called Umunwadim and the upper parts of Ngo and Ifite. Unfortunately, however, people hesitate to disclose such for fear that they might have their land and property confiscated for such research. A man was once said to have disowned some bead found in his farmland and refused to point at a spot where it was got. It will therefore, need a government force and wealth to evacuate the occupants of these areas and bring to a completion, the archeological works begun by Thurstan Shaw in 1959. I have written about the information about a wall that encloses a large area in the past, a wall that was said to have enclosed parts of Igbo-Ukwu, Azigbo, Awka-Etiti, Amichi, and Ogbodu near Ekwulu-Mmili. The fabrics of this wall remain today. In 1979, when a grave was being dug near the wall in Amichi bout 30,000 beads (Ibili) were found. These beads are similar to some of those found in Igbo-Ukwu by Shaw.

Some other items. Source: Shaw 1977

Again, it is important to note that the bronze culture of Igbo-Ukwu diffused all through Igbo settlements and awareness needs to be put in the people to enable them recognize and bring together these cultures wherever they lie...

> Similar discoveries in some other parts of Igboland, especially Bende and Ezira, confirm that this bronze age might not be restricted to a few communities pointing to what has been referred to as an old rich and original culture.

Onwejeogwu (1975) is of the view that Igbo-Ukwu culture is a pan Igbo culture that is to say that it belongs to all Igbo speaking people, a cultural heritage that belongs to Igbo as a whole. Even though the pottery associated with the culture is distinctive, thick yellowish and generally has deep spiral or concentric grooves. This pattern of pottery could still be found today in several parts of Igboland. This pottery type, which indicates the extent of Igbo-Ukwu culture, covers quite a wide area. It beats the imagination therefore, why Onwuejeogwu should go ahead to attempt to bottle this great culture into an Eri vessel.

"Hartle has also found some pottery at Nsukka, which dates as far back as the 4500BC. Though not the bronze but corresponds to the speculation of one of the great scholars on Igbo culture that Igbo must have lived here for nearly six millennia. This speculation is based on the anatomical study of the pollen grains that are deposited in layers upon each other according to the time when agricultural practice began on these lands". The bronze in Igbo-Ukwu must be far older than the specimen of charcoal and burnt wood that was used by Shaw in dating the finds.

Other Archaeological Sites in Igboland Ogbodu-Aba

Ogbodu-Aba is a town in Isi-Uzo Local Government Area in Enugu State. Archaeologist who studied them to be burial chambers, which have a lot of similarities with the catacombs in Europe and North Africa and are very much in resonance with the Igbo-ukwu burial chamber, explains what were found in Ogbodu-Aba. These burial chambers were accidentally discovered by an earth-moving machine in an effort to reduce the gradient of obstructing high lands during a road construction there.

The people of Ogbodu-Aba like the Igbo-ukwu people have no idea of the chambers hence cannot provide any useful information. This demonstrates the age of this culture. It is also amazing that the Igbo people in the past were technologically equipped to build those burial chambers. The culture has not entirely died among the Igbo people of today. Certain aspects of this burial are still imbibed in burial ceremonies all over Igboland. The occurrence of a more sophisticated and elaborate burial chamber in Igbo-ukwu confirms the unity of Igbo culture and should dispel entirely the claims of Umueri over this culture.

Besides, I have earlier talked of an ancient wall around Igbo-ukwu, which enlaced so many towns including a town called Ogbodu, which used to live near the present location of Ekwulummili. This Ogbodu is almost extinct, perhaps due to social forces or natural migration to other areas. On the other hand Ogbodu-Aba points to the northern Igbo plateau as the starting point of the migration of their fore fathers. These two archaeological artifacts must have more underlying connections and belong to the same broad culture

Ugwuele Stone Age Site

Ugwuele is a town in Uturu Local Government Area of Abia State. Among the things found at the Ugwuele site are many hand axe and Stone Age tools. The indication is that Ugwuele site was probably inhabited about 50,000 years ago. The archaeologist who excavated the site (Anozie 1987) believes it to be an Achuelian site. "Achuelian period is a period in history when man used stone tools known as hand axes and cleavers for hunting and gathering animals. The human species associated with the Achuelian culture is the Homo erectus and is believed to have been prevalent about 500,000 years ago."

However, the speculations on the age of the finds at Ugwuele are only assumptions based on the nature of the tools and its similarity to the Achuelian culture which is a culture named after the site of St Achuel in France where the culture was first found. There is no proving yet that this level of human development was taking place simultaneously in different parts of the world, so that any occurrence of similar culture is tied to that age. I think that what was found in Ugwuele still need a lot to be done on the dating, though it should be treasured in the mind that people may have lived here thousands of years ago which is still a good explanation for the distinctive development of the Igbo people.

Lejja Iron Age Site

Lejja is a town in Nsukka Local Government Area, just about 14km south of Nsukka town. An archaeologist in the Department of Archaeology in the University of Nigeria Nsukka found the Archaeological artifacts in Lejja. He brought his report in 1980 after his visit to the area. He noticed during this visit, some heavy cylindrical lumps of iron slag in a village square (Otobo) Realizing the importance of the iron slag he brought his finding to the University Department of Archaeology.

Slag is a bye product of the smelting or reduction of iron. The smelting of iron ore occurs at a temperature of about 700 degree centigrade, which is below the melting point of iron, which is 1500 degree centigrade. To attain this temperature easily, a furnace or enclosure is required. In the smelting of iron, iron ore, which melts first, is reduced to a spongy mass of iron called bloom. This bloom because it is produced below the smelting point of iron is in solid form but the non-ferrous impurities come out in liquid form and are known as slag (Anozie 1997 pg120)

The presence of slag in an environment is an indication that iron was smelted in that environment since it could not have been transported over a long distance without the use of automobiles. This also helps to affirm the fact that the Igbo people knew the technology of iron works so many centuries ago. It also refutes the futile idea of looking for the import of such technological work found in Igbo-ukwu and other parts of Igboland. The theory that all the artifacts found in these archaeological sites are designed and cast east of the Niger and south of the Benue must therefore be right.

Source: Shaw 1977

Chapter Four

The Denouement

Igbo-Ukwu Culture in the African Context

Africa is one of the longest known continents of the world, but until the 19th century, only little was known about its interior. There were occasional penetration through the deserts by Arabian traders of the Middle Ages and invasion by immigrants from the East; but these people had very little to tell us.

Africa is a country of high plateau surrounded by a fringe of swampy coastal plains. The rivers that flow from the interior fall abruptly from the edge of the plateau to the coastal plains forming rapids and falls. They break up into numerous shallow distributaries, which carry their waters to the ocean across great deltas. Thus, they are of little use for penetrating the interior and navigators were not vastly experienced to pass these obstructions then. Secondly, the Sahara Desert, greatest desert in the world, cuts off North Africa, which has been known for long, from the interior. Another desert also lies between the European settlements in the South Africa and the interior. These are the main reasons, which made Africa the "Dark Continent" for so many centuries.

Africa was a "Dark Continent" to the Europeans and vice versa. How could Mungo Park be regarded as the man who discovered the River Niger when men for hundreds of years before him fished and swam in this river?

Many believe that the Negro is a man without a history (a past). Black Africa - Africa south of the Sahara Desert, on this view is a continent where men by their own efforts have never raised themselves much above the level of the beasts. David Hume, a popular French philosopher held the view that Africans had " No ingenious manufacturers among them, no arts, no sciences", and Trollope say of Africans, " No approach to the civilization of his white fellow creatures whom he imitates as a monkey does a man". These were part of the thoughts that incited the moves to "civilize" these "uncivilized" people and even within the time of contact with these people, a former Governor of Nigeria could write that "for countless centuries, while all the pageants of history swept by the African remained unmoved - in primitive savagery". As late as 1958, Sir Arthur Kirby, Commissioner for British East Africa, in London could tell the Torquay Branch of the Oversea League that "in the last sixty years- little more than the lifetime of some people in this room - East Africa has developed from a completely primitive country, in many ways more backward than the stone age".

"Africans, on this view had never evolved civilization of their own. If they possessed a history, it could be scarcely worth the telling and this belief that Africans had lived in universal chaos or stagnation until the coming of Europeans seemed not only to find its justification in a thousand tales of savage misery and benighted ignorance it was also, of course exceedingly convenient in high imperial times. For it could be argued (and it was indeed, it still is) that these peoples, history-less as they seem, were naturally inferior or else they were "children who had still to grow up". In either case, they were manifestly in need of government by others who had grown up". (Basil Davidson 1961 P.20)

These were part of the belief that informed "the inarticulate major premise", the tendency of believing in an inherent African (Negro) inferiority. With the beginning of invasion and penetration of Africa, whenever anything remarkable or inexplicable turned up in Africa, a whole galaxy of non-African (or at any rate non-Negro) people is dragged in to explain it. The Phoenicians are brought in to explain Zimbabwe in Rhodesia.

The Egyptians are produced as the painters of the "white lady" of the Bradbury in South-West Africa. Greeks or Portuguese are paraded as the inspirers and teachers of those who worked in terracotta and in bronze in medieval West Africa, even the Hittites have had their day (Basil Davidson 1961 P.31).

This view of African achievement has so far changed and the desires to falsify this belief inspired the works of writers like Davidson. With the new light shed on Africa by such works, every one of the achievements of the African and other phenomena are generally agreed to have had a purely African origin. Writing against the so-called "inarticulate major premise", Davidson contends "this premise has no foundation in the facts, neither for ancient Africa nor for relatively modern Africa. Evolution and development in Africa, as elsewhere, have major key not in racial but environmental circumstance and there is nothing in the world to show or suggest that Negroes, had they lived in North Africa instead of Central Africa, would not have "done as well" or as "ill" as the largely Hamitic Egyptians and Berbers of the Nile valley and the Mediterranean shore".

Surprisingly, the work of Thurstan Shaw on the archeological findings from Igbo-Ukwu in the 1970s was still very much influenced by "the inarticulate major premise". This bias prompted Shaw into looking for the explanations to these enigmas outside Africa (Negro).

The description of the three objects found in the excavations according to Shaw are referred to as being made of Bronze and some being made of copper. The word bronze as used here means an alloy of copper, tin and lead or an alloy of copper, brass and zinc. This is because bronze and brass do not occur naturally and are only artificially made by man. Copper is comparatively soft and easily worked whereas brass and bronze are much harder. These components of the bronze are much harder. The components of the bronze found in Igbo-Ukwu would have given us a clue to the import except that there were no comparative records of such exports in Africa. However, through the most effective emission spectroscopy, the analysis of the coppery objects from Igbo-Ukwu were interestingly found that the majority were of a heavily leaded bronze, containing up to 12% of tin and up to 16% of lead, copper making up the rest. Some other objects were pure copper.

Shaw's premise was nowhere near to the idea that these objects could have been made here in Igbo-Ukwu, but he was able to affirm that "the interesting thing is that this division into objects of heavily leaded bronze and objects of almost pure copper correspond to differences in the technique by which they were made. Leaded bronze was used for those made by the lost wax casting process, whereas the object made by trusting, smithing, hammering and engraving were of copper, since bronze is better for casting and copper for smithing. It is clear that the ancient Igbo-Ukwu metallurgists knew what they were doing" (Shaw Thurstan 1977 P.72).

The scope of Shaw's research went outside Nigeria because reasoning on the source of the copper that formed the basis for most of these objects; there were no exploitable quantity in Nigeria particularly in ancient times. This was based on present reports. According to him, "the nearest source of copper is to the north of Nigeria in the region of the Republic of Niger. Ancient exploitation of copper is known near Akjoujk in Mauritania and around Nioro in the Republic of Mali. There is copper in Dar Fur in the western part of the Republic of Sudan and also in the Katanga and Zambia copper belt, but that is further away. Plentiful sources of tin are available within Nigeria, on and around Jos Plateau and it is known that the inhabitants before the advent of Europeans anciently exploited it. Unfortunately, we do not know how back this exploitation goes. There are lead and zinc deposits in South-Eastern Nigeria, which also show signs of pre-European exploitation. This raises the question whether the alloy used at Igbo-Ukwu was made in the area or whether it was imported from outside Nigeria in the same way that the copper must have been.

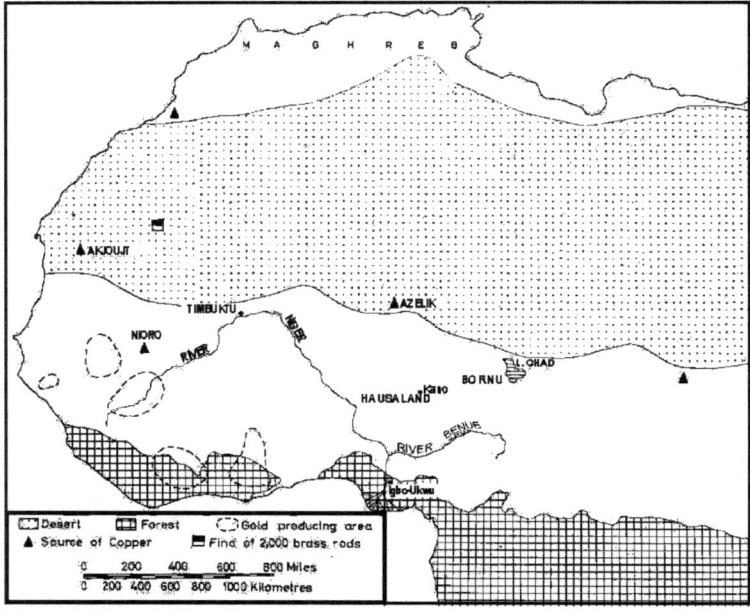

Map of West Africa showing the sources of copper and the spot in the Sahara desert where 2000 brass rods were dumped from a twelfth-century caravan

We do not really know the answer to this question but the fact that the source of lead in South-Eastern Nigeria is so closely associated with zinc and also the fact that there is virtually no zinc in Igbo-Ukwu bronzes suggest that the alloying was not done in this area. On present evidence, it seems likely that the Igbo-Ukwu bronze casters were importing copper from some source which they used for smithing and that from the source; they imported casting metal which they used for the last wax casting process (loc. cit.). There is a crossroad in coming to the conclusion that the Igbo-Ukwu bronzes were imported and not made here, how come the similarities in all the finds especially with regard to creativity, component and time? Do we also have to consign to accepting that they were imported already made from one source and within the same time? And if so, where? Perhaps, the article by V.E. Uchendu et al provides the best answers to these questions about the sourcing of the materials

Significantly as well, it is good to note that the bronze in Igbo-Ukwu has nothing or very little in common with the bronzes found in some other cultural centers in Nigeria. They differ in time, component, creativity and analysis. As Shaw notes, "a point of great interest in the difference in the metal composition of the casting from Igbo-Ukwu and those from Benin, only a hundred miles to the west on the other side of the River Niger, (It was Benin of course, which first made West Africa famous for its bronze.) Is that analysis has shown that the majority of the so-called Benin bronzes are in fact made of brass, containing a considerable percentage of zinc. The famous heads of Ife are different again, five being made of almost pure copper and a dozen being composed of leaded brass. (Loc. Cit.).

Whereas, there was a total absence of zinc and brass in the whole find in Igbo-Ukwu, a detailed analytical comparison between the find in Igbo-Ukwu and the finds in Ife and Benin is made by Thurstan Shaw in his work and all culminated in proving different sources to the materials and different artistic acumen coupled with a big difference in age and techniques. Though, there were a few similarities, these were not anything to count on. On the other hand, the Benin and Ife bronzes prove the same origin and have so much relevance to the Nok culture. They must be cognate cultures. Perhaps for the same reason, Thurstan Shaw's views were narrowed in his attempt to date these finds. Certainly, it was a Herculean task trying to date these objects, as they were older than the limit of local folk memory of the inhabitants whom Shaw sought information from. There was nothing to limit the date of the findings found within the excavation. Of course, he was looking out for objects that were dated with other cultures. The fiber of the textile that was found in Igbo-Ukwu was microscopically examined, without success in identifying it, except to say that it is not cotton. Its state of decay was also not guaranteed since textile is known to undergo no decay when placed so closely to bronze or copper. There is no presence of objects whose first appearance is dated in a neighboring culture, which can reasonably assure us that the finds excavated are not older than the import. This difficulty applied in its entirety to Igbo-Ukwu. None of the types of finds from the three sites were known from other dated sites.

In spite of the fact that beads were traded into Africa from outside for a very long time, it was extremely difficult to date finds with this because of the similarities in characteristics of different beads produced at different times and the lack of records on manufacturing factories' exports to Africa. It is good as well that Shaw noted himself that that was not all, that there were records of beads manufactured in Africa, which were not dated as well. About the other items like glass found in the digging, Shaw said, "Glass beads from Igbo-Ukwu have been analyzed by neutron activation and x-ray florescence showing that they are mostly made of soda-lime glasses with a few potassium glasses. This contrast with glass artifacts from Ife, which were mostly potassium glasses with some soda lime. A European origin is suggested for the potassium glasses, but the provenance of soda lime glasses is unclear, since the latter compositions are undiagnosed and could be consistent with European or Near Eastern Origin (Ibid).

Certainly, the allusions in Shaw's research must have been well understood by now. There are no doubts about "the inarticulate major premise" as being mainly his motive and hence, his concentration on finding the "import" without any considerations on the other hand that this culture or civilization may have been exported from this place. Significantly in the quest to find something to lay hands upon as to regard the dating of these objects, Shaw was able to affirm that "There is one interesting feature about the pottery at Igbo-Ukwu which may be an indication of date. In nearly all pottery making centers of Nigeria today, a common method of decorating pot is by use of roulette… The significant thing is that although the Igbo-Ukwu pottery is so highly decorated, roulettes have not been used at all" (Op. cit. P.85).

Roulettes can be made of any material having any desired designs and they are usually cylindrical objects. They are rolled under the palm of the hand over the surface of the damp clay thereby both consolidating it and leaving a negative impression of the design that is on the roulettes on the clay surface. Roulettes are known to be used in the pottery of Ife and Benin. The roulettes mainly used were of maize cobs, which were introduced into Nigeria at the advent of the Europeans, thereby enabling a speculation of the dates at 16th century. Where the absence of roulette on the Igbo-Ukwu pottery can only genuinely indicate an earlier date. This limitation of Shaw may have been refuted by the works of A. G. Hopkins, An Economic History of West Africa 1972 where he opined that maize came to Africa before European advent via the Mediterranean, across the Sahara, thus predating 16th century

In many other excavations in Africa, usually objects like smoking pipe, cowries etc occur which limit the dating of such to after AD 1650. But as a point of reference, the absence of such in Igbo-Ukwu finds may as well limit the age of these objects to before this time. Another object that presented an enigma to Shaw about Igbo-ukwu is the presence of the motif of a horseman hilt, which came from the burial chamber. This introduced a crossroad since from present knowledge; horses were not used in the area until lately. This is based on the speculations and case study of animals within the region. Horses are known to be in used Hausa land only from about AD 1000, which was about the time Arabian immigrants introduced it in this area.

However, for the failure to obtain any fact that would ensure a reliable speculation, Shaw had to base his dating absolutely on carbon dating. Carbon dating is the effective scientific means of dating objects (Details in Shaw's work). The result was very well in resonance with the extent of the speculations already carried on the objects. They dated up to the 9th century. The text for the accuracy being a confirmatory text on the two other deposits whose radiocarbon dates came very close on each other. Showing also that there was not much interval of time between them. From similarities between the three sites in the pottery, the metal works and beads there can be no doubt that the three sites belong to the same broad cultural tradition. Moreover, all the items disclosed in both the burial chamber repository and storehouse of regalia both display the same level of delicacy and complexity.

Quite good on another hand that Shaw was able to find out that apart from the motif of a horseman hilt, all the other motif of animals was that of animals found within the locality and thereby pre-establishing that these bronzes were made here in Igbo-Ukwu. The motif of leopard skull, the shell of snail, motif of curled snake, presumably a python, pendants designed as elephant heads, heads of ram, human heads, decorations in the shape of monkey heads, birds fish, beetle, spider, grass-hopper, snake, frog, snake holding an egg, snake swallowing a conventionalized lizard, pangolin, fly etc. Shaw was also able to identify the roped pot as an age long traditional way of making pots (ite-otu) for palm wine or a pottery vessel used as a resonator in dance orchestras (Udu) which are all still in vogue in the area.

There are other items such as the pedestal pot and the decorated open work panels of the altar stand which are made in the form of (Okpoga) small stool used for domestic work, which is still found in the culture. The ichi mark found in the faces of the human heads from the find I have dilated very well upon should dispel the myth of foreign origin. There are other motifs such as decorated bronze bowls and crescentic bronze bowl which the forms are still found in the "Oku" and in the "Agbai" still in vogue around the area.

The bifurcating motifs are also tropical motifs while the python has some important religious affiliations; killing it either accidentally or intentionally, is viewed as a taboo in the area.

Perhaps, part of what informed the "oriental hypothesis" and the searches for interpretations outside this area are the following reasons. First, there is the discovery of the soda-lime glasses in the Igbo-Ukwu finds, which diagnostically could be consistent with European or near Eastern origin. Secondly, the Igbo-Ukwu bronzes were not consistent with any previous finds in West Africa. Perhaps, it was assumed innocently that culture cannot develop independently or at least make its own contribution to a copied culture. Again, the best knowledge could only tell of an ancient manufacture of bead in the East.

Thirdly, the copper spiral snake ornament that are driven into the end of a wooden staff are excavated in the same location where the big bronze pots with dried leaves in them were also placed in positions that might suggest an important implication. Even though the dried leaves could not be identified, the whole setting of the objects suggests some medical purpose. Certainly, we know of the ancient culture of Hippocrates of Egypt, the founder of medicine, the symbol of which is a spiral snake mounted on wood and which medical doctors world over still use. We have also the documented records of the mount sin culture or the fiery serpent made of bronze by Moses in the Jewish tour of the wilderness (Number 21 4:9). " That whoever is bitten by a serpent and looks up to it shall not die". In addition to this, the spiral copper snake ornament has an egg in the mouth, which is a symbol of life. All these ideas are considered to be consistent with the Nubian culture.

Fourthly, the burial chamber in Igbo-Ukwu could have been copied from Nubia or Egypt where the burial of kings is very elaborate. We read of the mummification and majestic burials accorded to the Pharaohs from the Pypri and other sources.

Fifthly, the presence of the horseman hilt also opened a speculation that is consistent with the East. Arabians we know made very much use of horses as a beast of burden. Horses on another hand (according to previous understanding) were not known to be used in West Africa until about 1000AD when, they were introduced in Ghana and Northern Nigeria by Arabian traders. It beats the imagination then when it is realized that the import of this motif is much older than this. Speculations therefore ended up pushing the beliefs further to the East. Speculation on the triton shell (Chariona) which assumed to be represented in each case in the bronze casting of shell only pushed the conclusions further in this direction since this shell evidently abound near the Red Sea and on the Eastern part of the Mediterranean.

The Oriental Illusion

The allusion to the oriental hypothesis, which some modern authors embrace, did not begin with the work of Shaw. Perhaps Olauda Equiano was the first to make speculations on the oriental origin of the Igbo people, in the last two decades of the eighteenth century. (Equiano 1794 P.25-28). It is however, important to note that Olaudah most probably did so because of the cultural crisis he faced first as a slave and then as an ex-slave in the West Indies and in Britain, facing every kind of racial discrimination, and probably because the Jews at times were believed to be a race occupying a higher level on the history of mankind. Olaudah presumed that he could increase the importance of the Igbo race by linking it to that of the Jews.

After Olaudah's allusion came the British colonial officers who became interested in Igbo cultural history partly for scientific reasons, partly, to provide explanations to certain mental, psychological, linguistic and other traits which they considered peculiar to the Igbo and partly, to understand the Igbo and their society as a first step towards developing suitable institutions for governing them. Hence, it was borne out of the desire of the British to rule the Igbo conveniently. These groups of researchers were agreed on their methods and conclusions though not entirely always so on their aim until about the mid-1940s. Their methods were mainly dependent on cultural-traits chasing, looking for findings and isolating those aspects of Igbo culture, which they believed, gave some indication of either the origin of the people or of their culture or both. In the exercise of such traits as circumcision, the system and manner of naming children, sentence structure and similarity in word sounds, dual organization, religion in general and sun worship in particular, ritual symbolism and so on have been frequently used. Generally, both groups have come to the conclusion either that the Igbo came from the orient or that their culture evolved under the influence of a small elite of culture carriers from there. Two places in the orient were usually favoured; Egypt and the Holy land (Afigbo 1975).

M.D.W Jeffrey was also impressed in the same manner, by the Igbo sun worship as by the feature of dual organization in their social structure. He therefore held that the Igbo at some stage in the past came under Egyptian influence, the carriers of this influence being probably the Nri of Awka in Northern Igboland. (Jeffrey 1946 P.25ff).

Some other Igbo authors followed the same trend of thought in their works on Igbo origin, For instance, Ike in his work in 1951 asserted that the Igbo were originally Hebrew or a branch of the ancient Egyptians (Ike 1951 P.1-14).

Mathew also holds this view in his work of 1926. The only significant difference between the views of the indigenous writers and their European counterparts was that the European went no further than to assert that the Igbo came under the impact of either the ancient Egyptians or the Jews. In modern times, many writers on the Igbo history have also held to the oriental hypothesis to the extent of finding and establishing biblical linkages and similarities in the Igbo culture and the Jewish culture. But critical thinking has helped to make some logical conclusion on the motives of such claims. Equiano's claim, for instance, was based on his primary concern with the problem of the dismal lot of the black-man vis-à-vis the white-man, his utter importance in the face of Europe, his enslavement and exploitation, his humiliation in slavery, his misery and poverty. It was partly in attempt to refute the alleged superiority of the Europeans over Igbo that he made the claim of Jewish ancestry for his people and thus was able to affirm the inborn ability of the Igbo to rise to the level of the Europeans.

Colonialism was a severe humiliation for the Igbo, and for black Africa as a whole. The African predicament forced a series of efforts on the Igbo early writers to reaffirm their integrity. To show that they have not always been as despicable as the colonialists alleged, they therefore laid claim to oriental origin on the basis of such cultural similarities. At this time, historians thought that the orient was there to civilize mankind. The Igbo through the claim to oriental origin came to assign themselves a higher place in the history of the world than they would even assign to their British masters.

In spite of these realizations, many Igbo still make allusions to the oriental origin from the point of view of the social factors that pertain to the Igbo in the Nigerian context. The British colonialists amalgamated Nigeria in 1914. There are about 250 ethnic groups in this amalgamation with different languages, cultures and histories. There are three major ethnic groups of which Igbo are one because of their number. In contrast to the other ethnic groups in this amalgamation who were centrally organized, the Igbo came to Nigeria with their characteristic egalitarianism, individualism, competitiveness, taste for achievement, hard work and clamorous democracy (J.O.Oguejiofor). Under this colonial amalgamation, and partly for the population pressure, the Igbo came to see all parts of the country as a fair field for business and spread out in large numbers as traders, mission agents, government officials, migrant farmers and so on. "The wider area of operation offered by the Nigerian reality gave them the opportunity of putting into advantage personality traits that have sediment in them through the passage of centuries. The Igbo therefore, left their forest state and scattered far and wide in search of personal improvement in different areas of life. They are found in good numbers in almost every part of Nigeria. Typically, they arrive with nothing except their determination and their readiness to work. Typically, too, they make good within considerable short period of time but in their uncondescending tenacity and their boisterous attitude, they incurred the fear, envy, jealousy and sometimes outright hatred of the people among whom they live" (Oguejiofor J 1996).

Consequently, the Igbo became the victims of communal riots or threats of them wherever they went in Nigeria. Writers and other social publicists started drawing parallels between the Igbo people and the Jews for this reason. On the one hand are the Igbo business acumen and their suffering at the hands of other Nigerians ethnic nationalities and on the other hand is the Jewish experience throughout the history as we can at least read in the Bible. Another important point is the embattled Biafra between 1967 and 1970 when the rest of Nigeria teamed against the Igbo people in a war that presents a perfect parallel to the state of Israel surrounded by hostile Arab nations who occasionally team up against her. "The Igbo did not only make this comparison but believed in it. They also came to hope that they would weather the Nigerian storm just as the Israelis are weathering the Arab storm. Thus, there have been many enlightened Igbo whom the claim to eastern origin is neither mere history nor the oriental mirage of Salmon Reinach but an ideology for group survival" (Afigbo 1975).

According to Afigbo, by the late 1930s, the oriental hypothesis had been argued out and abandoned since no amount of research, not even Mathews' at Arochukwu and Jeffreys' at Awka could uncover solid historical or anthropological evidence in its support. In 1937, Dr. C.K. Meek, the government anthropologist who had coordinated the research into this and related issues in Igboland, closed the debate as far as the government was concerned when he warned that "No purpose will be served by engaging in speculations about ancient cultural contacts, such as that the prevalence of sun worship, of forms of mummification and of dual organization point to some distant connection with ancient Egypt. As far back as we can see within historic times, the bulk of the Igbo people appear to have lived an isolated existence (Meek 1937 P.5).

According to Afigbo, he was disgusted that in spite of the warning of Meek against applying the oriental hypothesis to Igbo cultural history, since he found out that his work on the Jukun was largely responsible for this error, unofficially and privately though, M.D.W Jeffrey continued to push the hypothesis through his publication on Igbo ethnography (Afigbo 1995). Igbo writers have also neglected this warning and have up to this modern time reacted to their predicament by presenting histories that bear strong inclination to the oriental hypothesis.

In this era, the scientific and critical question that should boarder on the oriental hypothesis should have been firstly; why in the first place was the oriental hypothesis imported as an explanation of Igbo History? The answer to this question may be very simple when one considers the fact that the anthropological studies made by the colonialist were founded on their desire to understand and hence rule the Igbo efficiently. This was because the colonial government was experiencing great difficulty in the administration of the Igbo. They set out to discover traditional structure of leadership, which they could utilize. It was on this ground that it came to be argued firstly that Igboland was once under Egyptian influence, secondly, that the spread of the Egyptian culture in Igboland was the work of a small elite who after inter-breeding with the people became the Nri and the Aro of today. The final question now becomes; if the colonialist discovered these structures to be right, why then did they not go ahead to rule the Igbo people through the Arɔ or Nri people? Why did they have to abandon this hypothesis? Why did they not go beyond suggesting oriental influence to oriental origin as Igbo writers themselves do today?

Secondly, if we are to judge the oriental influence or origin of the Igbo on the basis of such similarities in cultural traits such as sun worship, circumcision, mummification, the concept of God etc, what do we have to say about the basic distinction on leading and fundamental cultural principles? Such as

(1) The calendar system:

Unlike the Babylonians, the Greeks and the early Romans, the Egyptians and the cultures of the Nubians based their calendar upon the sun alone. As the earliest great farming civilization, Egypt was dependent upon annual flood of the Nile which brought water and rich silt to the rivers flood plain. Life in Egypt was controlled by the season and hence by the sun. The moon played no part in the calendar. The Egyptian year had twelve months, each having thirty days plus an extra five days at the end of the year. These five days were associated with the birthdays of the greatest gods of the Egyptian pantheon and were given over to cerebration.

On the contrary, we see an Igbo calendar that is based on a lunar calendar. Many authors have already written works on this calendar system so there is no repeating here, but one as a practical instance may have to consider the priestly function of Ezeulu in "Arrow of God" as a custodian of the calendar in the first chapter of the work. On the other hand, one may begin to see a correspondence with the Jewish calendar, which was a lunar calendar. Like the Igbo, the crescent moon marked the beginning of the month. Moreover, Nisan was the first month of the Jewish year, which was arranged so that the New Year began at approximately the spring Equinox whereas the Igbo calendar year was chiefly an agricultural technology, which begins with the planting season.

However, if we are to consider the similarities between these principles without having to look at the fact that every person can view the moon from any part of the world and has a capability to derive some underlying astrological fact from it, what do we have to say about the daily cycle? As in Judaism, which gave birth to Islam, the seven-day circle of days of the week marks the basic period of the work, rest and communal worship? In the Bible, the creation of the world takes six days and God rested on the seventh day. The Igbo have four days in the week namely; Nkwo, Eke, Oye, Afo and eight weeks in the month which only correspond with some African cultures and makes an allusion to the early Roman calendar that has eight days in the week.

(2) The Techniques:

The techniques used by Easterners raises a lot of questions about its contact with the Igbo civilization. What could be said about the absence of writing techniques, for instance, which developed so many centuries B.C. in the Eastern part of the world and was transmitted from this point to other parts of the world? Linkages are presumed from the presence of agricultural practices such as irrigation but the techniques of these practices were never the same and unfortunately based on the assumptions that the Igbo have no ideas as to develop some efficient means of farming. Attention is not paid to other techniques and practices of the Egyptians such as the ploughs that are pulled by animals, the storage system of wheat and other crops, etc.

The people of Meroe in lower Nubia developed hieroglyphic script, which up till today can be read but not understood. Attention was not paid to what was the social nature of the "divine kingship" in these sister cities before they were linked up with the Igbo. With the traces of divine kingship in Igbo culture, how did the Igbo develop a clamorous democracy that could even be viewed to be more advanced than that of the Greeks? Was there any trace of such democratic practices among the Orientals? How then did some writers and anthropologists on the Igbo culture see only the divine kingship as the leadership structure? How were the two, both divine kingship and clamorous democracy, compatible in one culture?

(3) The Morphology:

Finally, and most importantly, where is the morphological basis on which to base an argument on the oriental hypothesis? History and anthropological works have exposed the realities of some hermitic presence in the African population. However, according to Davidson, "These hermits have a white morphology. They go back it seems to the "Caucasian" stocks, which also produced most Europeans, though so, long ago that any reading of modern Whites and Blacks into ancient hermits and Negro would be singularly meaningless (Davidson 1961).

Some West African people have retained the characteristics of a white morphology. Notable among these and perhaps most important among them are the Peuls and Fulbe who live today in many scattered fragments and appearances throughout the western Sudan. Others like the Soughay have become or always were characteristically Negro (Loc.cit.). In Nigeria also, the Fulani have the hermitic morphology with their history traced to the collapse of Koumbi Saleh or ancient Hamitic settlement in Ghana. They still bear evidence of the Caucasian origin in spite of mixing with the local population in ancient Ghana, Mali, and here in Nigeria. Miscegenation could not wipeout this entirely. However, the Igbo oriental hypothesis has no such basis to back this speculation. A clear investigation on the faces from the archeological finds at Igbo-Ukwu, which was as old as before the 9th century, gives no evidence to this hypothesis. Logically, if miscegenation or interactions with the environment have brought the Igbo to bear much of the Negro morphology, one would most expect that the effect would be less on the ancestors who lived one thousand years ago. Unfortunately, the nose, for instance, on the faces of the human portraits from Igbo-Ukwu was even more Negroid type than the nose on the faces of Igbo-Ukwu people today. Qui da casu? These faces also bear tribal marks, which are only consistent with the Igbo cultural area.

In considering the Hamitic or oriental hypothesis in dealing with the Igbo culture, we should therefore reiterate the solemn warning of Levi Straus that " we should know only certain aspects of a vanished civilization and the older the civilization, the further are those aspects since we can only have knowledge of things which have survived the assaults of time. There is therefore a tendency to take the part for the whole and to conclude that since certain aspects of two civilizations show similarities, there must be much resemblance in all aspects. Not only is this reasoning logically indefensible in many cases, it is actually refuted by the facts (Levi Straus).

Negroes of Africa

Many anthropological and historical works have been done in Africa one of which is that of Professor Raymond Dart. He exposes the fact that Africa might hold the answer to the earliest development of man himself, which is suggested by evidence from East Africa. Finds in East Africa (mainly in Uganda and Kenya) not only include the earliest evidence yet available of Homo Sapiens, thus leading to a claim by some anthropologists, so far not denied, that Africa was the cradle of humanity.

Much evidence has also popped up since then to prove this premise, both that presented by climatic sequence and fossils. However, their principle reason for thinking that Homo Sapiens occurred first of all in Africa is that stone tools have been recovered from deposits laid down during the earliest of these periods, whereas stone tools in Europe turned up only much later in the long sequence of European "glacial" and "inter-glacial", thus, tools found in Uganda may be the oldest tools ever found anywhere.

A detailed study of the Negroid race by Basil Davidson shows that sometime around 5000BC, new types of humanity appeared in Africa. The Negro or Negroid types were prominent among these. His earliest remains have come so far from much the same African latitude, a fossilized skull and some other fragments from a middle stone age site near Khartoun in the Sudan, and another skull and some bones from beneath thick clay at Asselar, about 200 miles North-East of Timbuktu in the Western Sudan. These Negroes, according to Davidson, undoubtedly multiplied in the years after about 5000BC. An analysis of about 800 skulls from pre-dynastic Egypt from the lower valley of the Nile, that is, before about 3000BC, shows that at least a third of them were Negroes whom we know, and this may well support the view to which a study of language also brings some confirmation, that remote ancestors of the Africans of today were an important and perhaps dominant element among populations which fathered the civilization of ancient Egypt. (Davidson B 1961).

The revelation of the French explorer of the Sahara, Henri Lhote in 1958 with a wonderful collection of copies of rock paintings and engravings present an illuminating aspect about the Negroid history of migration in Africa; " for here was human history on the grand scale, tier after tier of Saharan style that told of a bewildering succession of different peoples through uncounted millennia, ranging from marvelously sensitive pictures of animals to no less sensitive portraits. The word is not too strong of men and women; from scenes of wheeled warfare to scenes of pastoral peace: from gods and goddesses that surely came from ancient Egypt to mask and figures that just as surely did not. Many of them were the work of Negro peoples in a time that was probably not long before or not long after 4000BC (Loc.Cit).

According to Davidson, from such evidence as the one presented by Lhote, the empty centuries enlarge and echo with forgotten peoples. It had earlier been thought and the opinion is useful to an understanding of the complexities, which accompanied this peopling of ancient Africa- that the Sahara had known four main periods of habitation during its time of fertility. The earliest of these had been a hunting people who were eventually followed by a cattle keeping people and these last, on their successors, had acquired horses around 2000BC into this bare outline. Lhote had poured a wealth of new evidence, which brings it suddenly and wonderfully to life. Basing himself on recognizable variations of painting and engraving style, he suggests no fewer than sixteen different phases of occupation between the time of the hunting people and the time of the cattle keeping people (1961 P.29)

Davidson therefore discussed the various people in Africa ranging from the Bushmen or Boskopoid to the Negroes, or Negroid and then the Hamites who perhaps are Caucasians. These races had their different lines of migrations and fusions.

There is no doubt that the mingling of these races produced at some more or less distant times in the past the ancestors of a majority of modern Africans.

The myth of "Hamitic superiority" veiling as it generally has an "inarticulate major premise" that Negroes are naturally inferior people, has long been discarded. The art of bringing in Phoenicians, Egyptians, Greeks or the Jews to explain any remarkable or inexplicable culture or civilization that turned up in Africa has also become previous manners of thought. Since it has been found that the problems of backwardness and progress- even when and where it really exists, and are more than the illusions of Euro-centric frames of thought, cannot be explained along any racial lines. The key is mainly hinged upon environmental influences. This explains why it is found that even when African people have taken much from outside, at different times and places, their process of borrowing whether of techniques or beliefs have always undergone an adaptation, through environment and circumstances, with societies and cultures and civilizations which became specifically and uniquely African.

It has also been agreed among historians on the evidence that the Negro specie was first found around Khartoum and that the Negroes were essential part of the pre-dynastic Egypt from the lower valley of the Nile which dates about 3000BC. These Negroes were perhaps forced to move southwards by yet the environmental factor. Evidence proves that " some times before the fourth millennium B.C, the Sahara began to lose its fertility. Its great rivers running southwards to the Niger and eastward to the Nile and whose arid beds may still be traced in fruitless outline began to dwindle and perish. Its lakes began to disappear. Its people began to migrate elsewhere. There is plenty of evidence for this long disastrous change. Those earliest Stone Age Negroes of Khartoum - those who laid the foundation for much of the civilization of the Nile and manufactured pots even before pots were made in Jericho, earliest of the world known cities - lived beside a river, which rose in flood between 12 and 30 feet higher than it does today.... Even as late as the third millennium, large numbers of cattle are known to have been found grazing in the lower Nubia whereas Aekell says, desert conditions are so severe today that the owners of an ox-driven water wheel has difficulty in keeping one or two beast alive throughout the year (Davidson 1961).

Perhaps, the continued rise in global warning which has forced the depletion of the ozone layer is part of the reason why the Sahara has increased continually over the ages - but the exact reason of this desiccation are yet speculative. Our major concern here is that the Sahara began to offer a major barrier to human passage some 5000 or 6000 years ago; at about the same time that Negro people began to move and multiply and North African began to develop settled agriculture. Therefore, this point marks the period of the beginning of a stretch of barriers to human contact between the lands to the North and the lands to the South.

"North of this worsening desert, there was intense and seldom interrupted contact between all the developing societies and civilization of North Africa, the Middle East and the Mediterranean. South of the desert, there was more or less, unrestricted movement throughout the continental mainland, so that Negroes or Negroid people are found today in almost every part of it. But the South and the North were increasingly divided from each other. They developed apart. They developed differently. This broad truth (though) is subject to reservations. Contact between North and South were never completely severed. Raiding, trading and migration routes led southwards from the Fezzan to the Niger, or coast-wards down the red sea and round the Eastern Horn of Africa. Carthage traded down to the Western Coast, though Phoenician secrecy has stopped posterity from knowing how much or how far. Horses and chariots were common in the Sahara for several centuries after about 1200 BC and later on there were the camel" (Davidson P.33).

Igbo People of West Africa

Few of the writers on Igbo history have considered the issue of the evolution of the Igbo culture; have done so taking fully into account the very important factor of interaction between the people and their environment. Few have also tried to build a history based on the archeological evidence found in Igboland. Among these few are Mr.G.I. Jones, who sought to explain the Igbo village planning in terms of Igbo agriculture and Igbo social structure in terms of the ecology at least with respect to the social structure of the central and North Eastern Igbo (Jones 1945 and 1961)

Afigbo went further than any in analyzing the culture by eschewing all kinds of narrowness of thought and discarding the oriental hypothesis and building a history on the given facts of culture. Interpreting the view of certain scholars, he placed the Igbo homeland somewhere further north, probably in the region of the Niger Benue confluence. (Henderson 1972, P.39).

According to linguistic scholars, for instance, it was most likely here that speakers of the member language of the Kwa linguistic sub-family of which Igbo is one, separated from their ancestral stock and moved out to occupy their present locations. Many members of the sub family are found in Nigeria. A study of their artistic traditions has also led art-historians to draw attention to the likely primacy of this general area of the Niger Benue confluence in the early history of these peoples. (Rubin, 1971 P 113-123 in Afigbo 1975).

Afigbo subscribed to the conclusion of Dr. Yehuda Karmon that the Igbo probably originated somewhere further north than their present habitat in the Sub-Guinea zone of the middle belt region of Nigeria, where they multiplied rather fast before invading the forest region where they then made their home (Karmon 1966 P.28-29). Again, Afigbo in his attempt to date this origin agreed with professor Robert Amstrong who using grotto-chronological evidence suggested that the members of the Kwa linguistic sub-family started separating from their ancestral stock between five and six thousand years ago (Amstrong 1962: P.284, 1964; P.22-23). He also observed that this estimate has been greeted with skepticism in a few quarters (Henderson, 1972; P.39) but by and large, that scholars are becoming more and more impressed with the ambiguity of the societies concerned as with their stability over the centuries. Thus, one would say, taking into account other cultural data that Professor Amstrong's estimate is not off the mark.

According to Afigbo, "on the strength of what evidence we now have, one can say that the upper limit for when the Igbo started emerging as a distinct people with a characteristic language, is about six thousand years ago. This conclusion would appear to be reinforced by the findings of preliminary archeological research in Igboland. Professor Hartle's work has shown that by the early Neolithic period, Igboland was under occupation (Hartle, 1969 P.134-143). Whether however, there was a break in occupation between then and now, or it has been continuous is still to be established by further work. However, the result of some test excavations at Nsukka (Northern Igboland) as well as the analysis of the materials recovered would seem to reveal a degree of ethnographic continuity in the area as to suggest that the ancestors of the Igbo were already living in the parts of present day Igboland at least by the third millennium B.C (Hartle 1967) in Afigbo 1975).

This conclusion of Afigbo seems by any academic standard to be the nearest to the probability about the Igbo origin. But a pertinent question that is posed to this conclusion is that given by the archeological find from Igbo-Ukwu. According to Strides, "...works at Igbo-Ukwu in eastern Nigeria where there is definite evidence of early iron smithing and a fairly sophisticated technology. Bronze casting of great beauty has been found and it is thought that they were made around AD 600. These bronzes are in a completely different style from those produced by the craftsmanship of Ife and Benin (Stride G.T and Ifeka C; 1971 P.112).

Stride also thought that the craftsmen are likely to have inherited their skills from forest peoples who worked metal and farmed before the migrant founders of the Yoruba people arrived somewhere around AD 1000. Thurstan Shaw also agrees that the soda-lime glasses with a few potassium glasses from Igbo-Ukwu contrast with the glass artifacts from Ife, which were mostly potassium glasses, but with some soda lime. He also agrees that the bronzes from Igbo-Ukwu differ both in component, creativity and techniques from other known bronzes of West Africa (Shaw 1964). How then do we reconcile the distinctive development of the Igbo people from the other Kwa-speaking peoples of West Africa?

With evidence, the appearance of iron in what is now Nigeria coincided with the ending of "Nok figurine culture" the last stage of which were probably transitional. New ideas and new technique, that is to say, stimulated the growth of new societies (Davidson 1961).

According to Davidson, Nok is a village of the Jaba people of Zaria province, where a couple of human heads in pottery were recovered. They were smaller than life size and appeared to have no connection with any culture that was known to have existed in the neighborhood. Three others were found in 1944, together with models of a human leg and foot, also in well-fashioned pottery and a complete cooking pot. Then the same year, Bernard Fagg recovered a splendid pottery head at Jemaa, some 24 miles from Nok village. Since then, a great number of specimens of the Nok figurines culture, as it soon came to be called, have turned up in a wide area, reaching for some 300 miles across the broad east-west valley that is made by the Niger and the Benue above the confluence of those great rivers. Many live size or near live size heads and busts, it should be noted, are among them. The likelihood now is that this interesting and advanced culture modeling its thousands of heads and stylistic figures was spread widely across Nigeria and perhaps beyond (Op.cit. P.65).

The astonishing heads and busts from Ife and Benin and some other cultures of West Africa, were found later to have been fathered by the Nok figurine culture. The Igbo-Ukwu finds proved to be an exceptional case. Perhaps, the tendency to look towards the Benue region is the thought about the Jukun of Benue River in Nigeria whose divine kingship culture recalls the divine kingship of Kush and Egypt. This divine kingship reoccurs in the Igbo culture and both are far from being alone in that respect as the culture spreads far into the Kwa people of West Africa. Also, we find the interplay of worship of divine rams and other cultural interplay. These traces of cultural interpretation can be many times multiplied and are fresh proof of that great unity in diversity, which gives so much of African culture its characteristic quality of resonance, complexity and age. It must be treasured in also the mind that these cultural interpretations may only have developed as a result of contact in the Igbo situation. For instance, the divine kingship had risen about 1400AD among the Eri, precisely in Aguleri, which is an outer frontier of Igbo territory and had only penetrated the hinterland from this point. It was only gradually diluted and eventually swallowed by the much developed and antecedent Igbo culture of rulership. The ram worship on the other hand was most prominent among the Aro who live on the outer frontier where they made contact with the Jukun. We also see the kingship structure absorbed by the Western Igbo people, which is a result of contact with the Benin on the Western Frontier of the Igbo territory.

The source of the copper found in Igbo-Ukwu may also present an important question as copper is not known to be found anywhere in Nigeria but in dealing with these considerations, we must note well the salutary warning of Piggott that "Archeological evidence alone at best affords grounds for tenuous inferences and at worse for uncontrolled guess work"(Piggott 1965 P.231-232).

The second question that wonders on the conclusion of Afigbo on the Niger-Benue confluence for the origin of the Igbo is on the settlement pattern of the Igbo. According to Afigbo, the northern Igbo area occupies a place of first importance in the story of the emergence of Igbo culture. From all the available data, it was the first place to be settled by the Igbo after they came into the forest, it was there that they evolved a distinct culture, it was from there that they moved out to occupy the other areas they now inhabit (Afigbo Op.cit P.36)

In his study of the Igbo early settlement, Dr. Karmon came to the conclusion that the Igbo in general tend to avoid watercourses; eroding surfaces of slopes and clayey soils, which tend to be waterlogged. If the people had their ancestral homes near the confluence of the two great rivers, why should they later avoid waterlogged areas and slopes? Why did they go out for steppes and high lands? What was their primary occupation and interest? Were they pastoralists, hunters or farmers?

According to Herbertson, "the earliest description of steppe scenery is found in scattered phrases of Holy Scripture which acquire a new meaning when this is realized. The desire of the shepherd king for green pastures and still waters represents the ideal of well-being in a steppe land, where water is often so scarce that man and beast are parched with thirst and the grass withers in the scorching sun. The thought of the shadow of a great rock in a weary land is nowhere so comforting as where the dry steppe is passing into the rainless desert, as on the borders of Palestine"(Herbertson).

Would that mean therefore that Igbo people were primarily pastoral? The answer to this question is not certain but could as well have an important implication. The best suggestion of the early occupation is perhaps contained in the Eri mythology. According to this story, after Nri had obtained yams, cocoyam. Oil palm tree and breadfruit tree from Chukwu, the neighboring people brought him livestock and other forms of wealth in exchange for food crops (Onwuejeogwu M.A in Isichei, 1978).

However, Afigbo went ahead to project reasons why he has held onto the primacy of Igbo settlement on the escapement and which in his view lies in the Northern part of Igbo settlement. This coincides with the view of the primacy of Agbaenu culture. However, Afigbo would rather prefer to call this area the Nri-Awka and Orlu axis. The reason why he prefers to use this terminology is best known to him and why he bridged the Nri and Awka are not well known. Perhaps, it is that same vice that is inseparable from every historian, the desire to bring to focus his own state. Precisely, Afigbo was talking of Agbaenu and its confederated states of which Orlu, Nri and Awka lie at the different frontiers of its territory.

According to Afigbo, in this area, investigations rarely come across traditions of movement from any area outside this plateau region. In fact, most of the communities claim to have moved in from a short distance away.........it is relevant that most of other Igbo groups claim that their ancestors lived originally on the Northern Igbo Plateau before moving out in search of unoccupied land. As will be shown later, most of the movements would appear to have originated from Nri-Awka and Orlu areas.

This in any case is the Igbo explanation for the eminence of Nri and Amaigbo (Orlu) amongst them. Major A.G Leonard uncovered this fact in 1966, that is, within a few years of British penetration of the Igbo heartland (Leonard, 1906 P.11-47). Starting from this and analyzing the claims of descent from the Awka-Orlu axis, Mr. G.I Jones has produced a pattern showing the process and stages of Igbo dispersal within the area they now occupy (Jones 1963 P.30). Jones and Leonard were not talking of Nri, Awka or Orlu per se but the areas that fall between these locations to which Afigbo made allusions as the Awka-Orlu axis.

Significantly, the peak of this plateau lies at Igbo-Ukwu and this place is also the central part of this location. It seems therefore beyond coincidence that the Igbo culture had its cradle at this point and that this place is primarily called Igbo.

The second reason, which Afigbo based on for suggesting the primacy of the Northern Igbo plateau in the history of Igbo culture, is ecological. "All the authorities that have considered this matter, scholars like Dr.Yehuda Karmon (1966 P.28-29), K.M Buchanam and J.C.Pugh (1969 P.35), G.I Jones and H. Mulhall (1948 P.11), P.A. Allison (1962 P241-249) and many others are agreed on the fact that what is now Igboland originally carried tropical rainforest vegetation but through intensive and extended human use, the vegetal cover has been reduced to derived savanna and palm bush. In explaining this vegetal deterioration, which was accompanied by soil exhaustion, people had laid emphasis on the density of population which has been compared to that of the Nile Valley (Karmon, 1966 P.5; Flint, 1966 P.63) poor means of soil conservation and so on". Afigbo also took into account the length of time during which the Igbo have lived on and exploited this part. The importance of this would be more obvious when it is remembered that the technology at the disposal of the Igbo for coping with this environment remained at a relatively primitive stage until very lately. Now, of all the parts of Igboland, the Northern Igbo area has lost its vegetal cover most. This would suggest that it has been under continuous Igbo occupation far longer than other parts (Afigbo, 1975).

He also drew evidence from the pattern of Igbo settlement, which in the conclusion of Yehuda Karmon, the Igbo in general tend to avoid watercourses, slopes, clayey soils and water logged areas. The reason he postulated for this pattern was chiefly agricultural and for health purpose. However, this would be correct if the Igbo people were first and foremost farmers.

Afigbo also considered the population of people in Igbo cultural areas. "The Northern Igbo area is the most elevated region of Igboland. Around it are relatively low-lying plains and river valleys which still carry denser forests and therefore which about six thousand years ago would have carried still denser vegetal cover. The population density on these plains is still far below what obtains on the plateau. The Cross-River plains are under-populated and from traditions are areas of later Igbo settlement. If the Igbo until lately, resisted the settlement of these low-lying areas in large numbers, it becomes easy to see why they would have settled first on the Northern Igbo plateau. It was then most likely to have been drier and less densely covered with forest than the surrounding regions. It thus offered better conditions for settlement for the in-coming Igbo. (Afigbo 1975)

Besides, "an analysis of the oral traditions of most of other Igbo groups reveals that this region after some time came under severe population pressure. One result of this was that hard-pressed groups soon left in search of unoccupied lands to the south, west and southeast of the area". Most communities have their history of migration from this area while those communities around the Northern plateau have no traditions of movement from anywhere or from far distant areas` outside this northern area.

The Phenomenon of Nri and Other Igbo Cultures

Many writers and researchers have been fascinated by the cultural heritage of the Nri in some parts of Igboland. Speculations and derivations have also been made about this culture the most prominent of which seems to be the works of Michael A Onwuejeogwu. However, just as to ask why an early civilization should have appeared in the Nile valley, the Near-East, Mesopotamia and not in Northern Europe or in Southern Africa may be an interesting exercise in speculation, so does the question on the rise of Nri seem. With present knowledge, it has become little so. River-valley cultivation seems to hold the clue.

According to Davidson, early civilizations all took their rise in great river valleys, and these no matter how much they otherwise differed, all had their peculiar characteristics of natural irrigation and soil renewal. Annually these rivers offered new soil, exceptionally rich for cultivation. This enabled nomadic man, then discovering the possibility of growing food rather than merely collecting or hunting it to turn from his nomadic life. In so doing, in settling in one place for several years at a stretch he was faced with the technical problems of regular cultivation. And in solving these problems, precisely where river irrigation annually offered new soil, he also solved the problem of growing surplus food.

And with the emergence of this hitherto unknown phenomenon of surplus food, there emerged the foundations of commerce. Trade was the foundation in turn for permanent settlement, permanent settlement meant specialization, the division of labour, and the growth of cities. The growth of cities meant civilization, the development of central government of the autocratic and often divine rule that was peculiar to Bronze Age Egypt and other ancient civilizations. (Davidson 1961)

Though some authors on Eri origin claim that they are of the same stock as the Igala, it seems that there was only a kind of culture contact between these groups, which does not have enough basis to dismiss the group as not being primarily Igbo. The Nri or Eri are most likely part of Igbo stocks that migrated earlier from the Northern Igbo plateau between the 11th and 14th century. The reason for the migration may be the same population pressure which according to researchers like Jones was already severe in this area by the 10th century. Many other Igbo stocks had migrated from this area within this time to the East, West and Southwest.

The Eri seem to have reached the Anambra River and had begun a settled life at this place. Just as the civilization of the Nile valley was not born out of a void but rather is a collection and synthesis of cultures and civilizations from the womb of Africa; so also is the Eri civilization in Igbo culture. "An analysis of some 800 skulls from pre-dynastic Egypt, from the lower valley of the Nile, that is before about 3000 BC. show that at least a third of them were Negroes or ancestors of the Negroes whom we know and this may well support the view, to which a study of language also brings some confirmation that remote ancestors of the Africans of today were an important and perhaps dominant element among populations which fathered the civilization of ancient Egypt". (Davidson pg. 28). The practice of sun-worship, of forms of mummification, of priest kingship, of medicine and of dual organization which point to some distant connection with ancient Egypt, as was premised by Davidson have actually been proved by the work on African culture to be contrary to the views that these practices were copied from Egypt. The attitude of holding to this ideology was finally abandoned in Igbo history after the solemn warning of Meek (1937 pg. 5), that "as far back as we can see, within historic times the bulk of the Igbo peoples appear to have lived an isolated existence".

The civilization of the Nri of which much has been written was definitely not born ex nihilo. In Egypt for instance, contrary to assumptions, it has been proved that there was no one-way traffic of cultural diffusion from the Nile valley to other parts of Africa. The Nile valley civilization was only a synthesis of cultures from within Africa and around the world, which was enhanced by the settled life. Nri or Eri settlement in the Anambra River Valley may chiefly be the reason behind the rise of Eri or Nri civilization, which was mainly an agricultural civilization, and this is evidently a synthesis of cultures prevalent in the Igbo mainland merged with the Igala's and western monarchy.

There is probably very little doubt that it was cultivation and the working of iron that enabled the Igbo to master their environment and evolve advanced social and cultural patterns. The priest kingship may now be understood as not copied from the Hamites but had its evolution in the Igbo culture and social developments. The Igbo had developed a distinctive social pattern, which perhaps was mainly enhanced by the population pressure and land demand. The priest king influence, are probably in their wane when the Nri, having migrated to the Anambra River, were strengthening the priest king structure with influences from the west (Benin) and the north (Igala). This culture is responsible for the organization of the Nri and is later, in the 17th century seen to have enabled the Nri to influence other Igbo areas. It is good to note here that there were similar priest king leaderships anciently, primitively spread around Igboland and built on the communities' deities but which has been mostly overridden by the evolving of ultra- democracy and egalitarianism. The democratic culture also seemed to have evolved due to the population density on the pristine settlement.

External influence from cultures like Igala, and Bini were responsible for the adoption of the kingship pattern of the Nri, just as some other western Igbo were influenced to do the same.

Now it is claimed that it was with the priest king of Nri, that the coming of cultivation is associated. Likewise is the Igbo staff of office and symbol of right conduct, "ofo", the Igbo facial mark "ichi", the Igbo four-day week "izu", etc. Contrary to this view, the work of Afigbo demonstrates that there is much more to this. He made a study of the role of agriculture in the development of Igbo culture.

According to him, land more or less became the center of Igbo existence. It was for them not only the most important economic asset but also the most vital and the most active spirit-force in their lives. As an economic factor it influenced Igbo socio-political evolution. Those communities who were able to work out some arrangement for the exploitation of the land on which they lived became 'brothers' and each group of 'brothers' by functioning as a land owning, land defending and land seizing federation became a political unit. It was as much as the Igbo could do to work out such arrangement up to the level of village group. For the Igbo, the village group thus became the largest political unit. Any grouping, such as the clan, which did not have land-administering function failed to become a political unit in the normal sense. Neighboring communities, which failed to work out an agreement for the exploitation of land never became 'brothers' and therefore never became members of the same polity. (Afigbo 1975)

I have argued earlier that the Igbo were very much settled and had a very well developed social structure before the advent of the Nri culture. It is not only that land influenced this evolution of the Igbo socio-political units; it also helped to determine their settlement pattern. This is because it was the key factor in agriculture. Consequent to this, land (ala), came to occupy a very important place in Igbo religion and cosmology. It was worshipped and rules known as "Omenala" were promulgated to protect land abuses and transgressions. Ala was the guardian of Igbo morality.

According to Afigbo, "The Nri of the Northern Igbo achieved ascendancy in most of Igboland by marking themselves out as people who enjoyed a special relationship with 'ala'. In this way they became the foremost manipulators of this rural agricultural world. Not only could they reveal and declare the wishes of 'ala', they could also intercede between it and any person or community that broke its injunctions as well as remove the pollutions 'nso' arising from such transgressions. The privileged position of the Nri with regard to the 'ala', the premier active deity of the Igbo, goes to strengthen the suggestion that Igbo culture originated in the Northern Igbo plateau. M.A.Onwuejeogwu, who has carried out extensive researches into this matter has even expressed the opinion that it was the Nri who originated the concept of 'ala' as a spirit-force and propagated it in the rest of Igboland (Onwuejeogwu, 1972 pg. 15-56). If that was so, then it could indeed be argued that they synthesized Igbo culture (Afigbo 1975 pg. 43).

The Nri civilization is therefore an important ground to count on while dealing with Igbo history but this is not to say the same while dealing with Igbo origin. Iron technology, which came after the Bronze Age, was not an Nri civilization but a civilization known throughout the Igbo settlements. The same could be said of the 'ichi' culture. The agricultural civilization, which according to Afigbo, is dated along with iron civilization was also wide spread in the Igbo settlements and only synthesized by the rise of Nri. Trade was also developed as a result of these developments, that is, the need for exchange between the iron producing; livestock and food producing; mineral producing etc. areas. Thus Igbo civilization, which according to Afigbo was an agricultural civilization, would appear to have been nurtured on the Northern Igbo plateau (Agbaenu) and is in its ramifications a culture belonging to the entire Igbo race. This culture is spread all over Igbo settlements.

Finally, I already elaborated on the cultural origin and migrations of the Aro and Ezechima together with other Igbo cultures of migrations. They all support the primacy of the Northern Igbo plateau and dispersal from this point. Most oral traditions also suggest an initial movement from this region, into the south by the ancestors of some of the present day southern Igbo (the Uratta, Ikwere, Etche, Asa, Ndoki, etc). Afigbo has treated the sequence of the Igbo dispersal, in his work of 1975. He also attempted at dating these dispersals and migrations, which perhaps is the most accurate account so far in producing a true Igbo history of dispersions and origin.

Conclusion

Contrary to the view that Igbo people originated from the Niger-Benue confluence region, a view supported by evidence from the historical origin and development of the Negroid race and the early distinctive development of the Igbo, one is persuaded to place the origin of the Igbo somewhere around Khartoum in Sudan. History has traced the earliest record of the Negroid existence to the Stone Age Negroes of Khartoum. These Negroes are found to have made great contributions in laying the foundations for much of the civilization of the Nile (Davidson 1961)

At about the same time when the Sahara began to pose as a major barrier to human passage about 5000 or 6000 years ago, the Negro people began to move and multiply and North Africa began to develop settled agriculture. (Ibid.) According to Afigbo, "On the strength of what evidence we now have, one can say that the upper limit for when the Igbo started emerging as a distinct people with a characteristic language is about six thousand years ago (Afigbo 1975). This conclusion would also appear to be reinforced by the findings of preliminary archeological research in Igboland. Professor Hartle's work has shown that by the early Neolithic period Igboland was under occupation (Hartle 1967 pg. 134-143)

The potteries discovered at Nsukka were dated to be made about 4500BC and the analysis of the material recovered would seem to reveal a degree of ethnographic continuity in the area, as could suggest that the ancestors of the Igbo were already living in parts of Igboland at least by the third millennium BC (Hartle 1967). This also proves to be a continuation of the works of the Stone Age Negroes of Khartoum who manufactured pots before even pots were made in Jericho (Davidson).

There are other characteristic developments that support the view on the Khartoum of the lower Nubia as the origin of the Igbo. These include; the prevalence of sun worship; forms of mummification; of circumcision; of the priest kingship; of the Mount Sin culture of Hippocrates (the origin of medicine); and of the dual organization which historians has for long seen as the basis to project the 'oriental hypothesis' of a Hamitic origin or influence. Evidence now shows that the Negroes did not copy these cultures from the Orient but perhaps the reverse may be the case; that these practices in and around Africa were only synthesized and advanced in the Nile valley. These practices are not only seen among the Igbo but in most Negro cultures.

The Igbo seem to have developed like some other Negro races near Sudan. The lines of the migration seem to have gone through the highlands of central Africa and between the Benue River and the Cameroon Mountains. There appears to have been a stopping point along the edge of the rain forest before the Igbo eventually multiplied and invaded the northern Igbo plateau in the rainforest of southern Nigeria.

Even though scholars have proved that the Negroes did not learn the art of ironwork from anywhere, the Igbo seem to have maintained an ancient trade link with the Sudan and other Saharan trade routes. The Igbo succeeded in transforming their environment using only simple tools, a deduction that could be made from the age and maturity of the Igbo-Ukwu culture, which also supports the conclusion that Igbo origin probably goes back six centuries

According to Afigbo, "a study of Igbo-Ukwu finds made by Professor Shaw (1970), would seem to reveal that by the 9th century AD, Igboland was already engaged in long and short range exchange trading. Long range exchange brought in such items as the horse, bronze and carnelian beads from markets in the Sudan and beyond. The short range or regional exchange helped to assemble the slaves and ivory which paid for these luxury goods, as well as collecting the worked bronze" (Shaw,1975)

This extrapolation may not be accurate since, according to Professor Shaw, even though it was unlikely that all the bronzes were cast at Igbo-Ukwu, from its distinctive styles and mortising, they were probably all cast east of the Niger and south of the Benue Rivers. (Shaw 1977). The provenance of copper and other materials used by the Igbo-Ukwu metallurgist only suggest a network of trade for materials and not that the master pieces were assembled from other master-craftsmen elsewhere. The evidence of ancient knowledge of ironwork still remains among the Igbo till date.

Thustan Shaw's work of 1977 also shows that there had been ancient manufacture of beads in Africa in periods that cannot be dated. On the other hand far from Shaw's conclusion that horses were not known in Nigeria and West Africa until 10th century AD, Davidson has succeeded in finding that horses and chariots were common in the Sahara for several centuries after about 1200BC and later on there was camel (Davidson 1961;pg 33).

The Igbo seem to have invaded the rainforest and settled on the northern Igbo Plateau about 5000 year ago. The peak and center of this plateau falls at Igbo-Ukwu where the most sophisticated of Igbo art and creativity and work on their environment was discovered. This area was probably the first to be occupied by the Igbo and has been heavily exploited. One of the evidence to this truth is the disappearance of the probably vegetation and the deterioration of the soil in this area. The population here seems to have grown very extensively. In this area, agriculture ceased to be very profitable and land was in high demand in the sense that food demands in this area were no longer met. The people responded to this situation by migrating to other areas where there was supply of fertile lands and minerals. These migrations were difficult since most Igbo despise low lands and water logged areas. There was initial migration into Udi highlands before eventually the population pressure and other demands forced some elements to adapt   to other environments. Those who did not migrate responded by taking to other professions such as trade, smithery, medicine, the running of oracles and so on. In other words, they developed specialised professions, which they peddled among the other Igbo cultural groups whose soils could still support profitable agriculture. In this regard, it is note-worthy that most of the famed traders and other specialists of Igbo land such as the Awka, Aro, Nkwerre, Abiriba, Nri, and so on are located on the Northern Igbo plateau and its south-easterly extension through Bende to Arochukwu (Afigbo 1975).

At the center of these areas famous for their trading lies a market called **"Nkwo Igbo"**. Nkwo Igbo as considered by many is the most ancient and popular traditional market that served the commercial need of the entire people in the past. Trade interests and migrations had gone towards the direction of this market in the past and somehow in the present. It is therefore no coincidence that the remains of the Igbo civilization and evidence of primitive trade links were found near this market.

Another factor that facilitated the development of trade around this area was the differential distribution of essential mineral deposits in Igboland. The northern Igbo plateau and its extension to Bende, according to Afigbo, is rich in iron ore deposits. It was here that smelting and iron working were most highly developed in Igboland. The iron tools and implements produced on the plateau were in great demand over the rest of Igboland and even beyond. On the other hand, in the North-Eastern Igbo area, there are brine springs and lead deposits which would appear to have been exploited from very early times. (Talbot 1927). There would appear to have been a demand for lead among the smiths of the Northern Igbo area. (Onwuejeogwu, 1972). While salt was in demand throughout Igboland, there was also demand for fish supply among the Northern Igbo area. This is because of the lack of rivers and ponds from which fish could be caught. Fishes were only got from the Niger or Anambra Rivers to the west or from Cross River to the east. The movement of these minerals and goods must have helped to stimulate the further development of exchange economy among the Igbo.

These trade developments are part of what reflects in the trade specialization of the Northern Igbo people of today. This trade specialization is still found among the Igbo people in the context of Nigeria. The Igbo are generally known for their business prowess in Nigeria, but among the Igbo people themselves, trade is most proficient and common among the Northern Igbo (Agbaenu). Though the population pressure and lack of support from the land may still be viewed as a key factor to this development, these are all parts of the same truth.

Epilogue

The motive of this work is not to rest any claim on the Igbo cultural tradition of origin, but to say what the Igbo cultural tradition is. This is a Herculean task, because no matter how vividly one approaches this, one cannot say conclusively that this is where the origin is. This is because of the absence of written traditions before recently and for the extent of time involved since we are dealing with a history beyond folk memory. The only goals assured to such a work remain the opening up of a new arena of inquiry and bringing the public closer to reality. This is because of the obscurity of this history.

However, no matter how obscure the history might be, we are at least at ease with some realities; that the history of the Igbo origin is complicated by migrations, confluences, bifurcations and diffusions. The components of the tribe are simply people of the same or similar cultural origins that migrated into the area at a particular time in history. They blended with the environment and grew very extensively. This growth and lack of support from the lands and the resources forced a continual dispersion and interaction with new areas. Memories became more eluded of earlier migrations in favour of more recent ones. Interactions with neighbours or external influence also forced some little disparity on the culture though not on its unity and coherence. Some other realities of the history forced the unification of diverse elements into most of the communities that survive to date. These facts also allude to the complexity of Igbo history. The task becomes finding by a comparative analysis, what the proto-Igbo culture was first and foremost. Knowing this and by the same comparative analysis, finding the principle and most primitive settlements, traits and morphological features of this people, we would be able to specify or perhaps speculate on the source region of this people.

Civilizations rise and fall. We can understand from analysis that the Igbo had built some great cultures in the past. These cultures were over-ridden by time and events. No other people or person can make a claim on this ancient culture except Igbo where the fabrics of this culture lie and are found surviving or revived in different forms. Some migrations of some Igbo elements that perhaps by foreign influence and adulteration were able to form political, religious or social unifications were part of later developments. The rise, contributions and influences of the solidarity of such groups are very much intact and handy that the least experienced chronicler would come to the minutest detail of its history. Beneath all these lies the more primitive history of settlement or in another term, a prehistoric settlement. The history of this settlement and dispersion for the age has grown so thin that virtually not many can stand to a challenge on a debate about this history. Fortunately, the nation still remains unified by the common names, cultures, religious beliefs, political, and social organizations etc., which prove a more anciently unified history to the peculiar and limited diffusion of later developments.

To most Igbo, this debate is no longer necessary since it is not very useful as an aid to their present quest. For this oversight therefore, some egotist and anti-egalitarian Igbo elements tend to cease on the lapse to undermine the entire Igbo history by presenting their much more secondary and subservient history and proclaim it the only history worthy of the name for the whole Igbo. Unfortunately, this has always come against a moving train, the truth of Igbo history, so it has always been rejected by most and reluctantly accepted by a few. The result is that the Igbo were assumed as a race without a history.

Fatigue has caused these deformities, and perversities, which have only given place for confusion and instability. This situation is so implicit that it has become necessary that this debate be taken up. If not for any glories, at least, for the sake of preserving the truth and as far as the future generations and the public at large are concerned, to avoid stepping into more hopeless state of hoodwinking. But above this, I feel that the Igbo people need to understand, through a work like this, their historical background, their sociological developments, the reason for their political, social, religious, and psychological behaviours and inclinations. This I believe would infuse into well-meaning Igbo citizens the need for us to eschew certain tendencies, realizing that we are one and should unite to face squarely the challenges of our world. The spirit of unity, brotherhood, chauvinism, and nationalism and not dispersion and antagonism is advocated by this work.

To pick up such a challenge, one must be very careful not to fall into error of falsehood, that is to say, fabricating false and baseless arguments or reasoning from a cage. Such a history should be wholly and entirely true and should be based on realities, which are indubitable. The truth quite indubitably exists and the facts abound, such facts as seen in the oral tradition, written works, folklores, archeological finds, characters, features and cultures etc. What remains is to make a veritable extrapolation from these facts. It therefore will beat the imagination, if future writers on this topic will still miss the point and write only on the periphery and if the many intellectuals of the Igbo origin still remain silent on this point and allow the crisis to linger on.

Therefore, in spite of the fact that I have come a long way to this level in expressing my views, I cannot yet put a period to this discussion. This work, therefore still remains open to additions and subtractions or even a general review or over-view of the entire work, hoping that this may not become an opportunity for a charlatan to put out the same product under a different signboard. I will also welcome any attack on this work, whether sincerely or wantonly made.

Bibliography

Achebe C 1985,	Things Fall Apart, Lagos, Heinemann Educational Books (Nig) Ltd.
Achebe C 1977,	Arrow of God, Heinemann London
Achebe, 1983,	The Trouble with Nigeria, Enugu, Fourth Dimension Publishers.
Afigbo A.E 1975,	In, Igbo Language and Culture; Oxford University Press, Ibadan.
Afigbo A 1985,	The Age of Innocence (Owerri Ministry of Information)
Afigbo A.E 1972,	The Warrant Chief; Indirect Rule in Southeastern Nigeria 1891-1929, London Longman Group Ltd.
Alison P.A. 1962,	Historical Inference to be drawn from the effect of human settlement on the vegetation of Africa: Journal of African History 3
Amstrong R.G. 1960,	The development of Kingdom in Negro Africa, Journal of the Historical Society.
Amstrong R.G. 1962,	Glottochronology and West African Linguistics, Journal of African History 2.
Anadi C.K 1972,	The Kingdom They Know not, Enugu Ochumba Press.
Anozie F, 1979,	West African Journal of Archaeology vol. 9
Anozie .F. *et al* 1987,	Discovery of Major Prehistoric site at Ugwuele Uturu, Okigwe Imo State. West African Journal of Archaeology vol. 8
Azikiwe N 1970,	My Odyssey; An Autobiography, London, C. Hurst and Company.
Bradbury R.E 1970,	The Benin Kingdom and the Edo People of Southwestern Niger (London, International African Institute)
Buchanan K.M and Pugh J.C. 1969,	Land and People in Nigeria, London
Buah F.K 1981,	The Ancient World, A New History For Schools and Colleges, Macmillan London.
Conrad Joseph, 1931,	The Secret Agent, Everyman Paperback, London.
Davidson, B. 1969,	The African Genius, Little Brown and Company, Boston.

Davidson, B. 1961,   Old Africa Rediscovered, Victor Gollancz Ltd, London

Donceel J.F 1961,   Philosophical Anthropology. New York Sheed and Ward Inc.

Dunn L.C 1975,   In: Race and Biology in Race, Science & Society. UNESCO Press George Allen & Unwin, Paris.

Echeruo M.J.C 1979,   A Matter of Identity; Owerri, Ministry of Information.

Echeruo M.J.C and Obiechina EN (eds) 1972,   Igbo traditional Life, culture and Literature conch Magazine Vol. III No 2 September 1972.

Ejiofor L 1982,   Igbo-Kingdoms, Onitsha, Africana

Engels Fredrick 1976,   Anti Duhing, Foreign Language Press, Peking

Equiano O. 1967,   Equiano's Travel; P Edwards (ed.) London Heinemann,

Fage J.D 1962,   Introduction to the History of West Africa. Cambridge University Press

Forde D & Kabemy P. 1976,   West African Kingdoms in the Nineteenth Century, London Oxford University Press.

German Sholom 1985,   The Theory that Transforms the World, Novosti Press Agency Publishing House Moscow.

Hartle D.D. 1967,   Archeology in Eastern Provinces by the Secretary for Native Affairs, Lagos.

Henderson R.N . 1972,   The King In Every Man, Yale.

Herbertson A.J & FD 1947,   Man and His Work, London & Co. Black Ltd.

Hopkins A.G   An Economic History of West Africa, 1972

Idigo M.C.M 1965,   The History of Aguleri, Lagos

Ifesieh E.I 1989,   Religion At the Grassroots, Fourth Dimension Publishing Co. Ltd. Enugu.

Ikenna N. 1972,   Studies in Igbo Political Systems; London, Frank Cass and Co Ltd.

Ike, A 1951,   The Origin of the Ibos, Aba.

Iloyd P.C. 1972,   African in Social Change, London, Penguin.

Isichei E. 1977,   Igbo Worlds, London, Macmillan

Isichei E. 1973,   Igbo People and the Europeans; London Faber and Faber Ltd.

Isichei E.A 1976,   Short History of the Igbo People; London, Macmillan.

Isichei E... 1970,   Igbo World.

Jeffreys M.D.W 1946,   The Umundri Tradition of Origin, African Studies, No.15

192

Jones G.I 1945,	Agriculture and Ibo Village Planning Farm and Forest.
Jones G.I... 1961,	Ecology and Social Structure Among the North Eastern Ibo Africa, No.31.
Jones G.I. and 1948, Mulhal	An examination of the physical type of certain peoples of south-Eastern Nigeria: Journal of Royal anthropological institute
Jordan J.P 1975,	Bishop Shanaham of Southern Nigeria, Dublin.
Karmon, Y. 1966,	A Geography of Settlement in Eastern Nigeria, Jerusalem.
Leiris M. 1965,	Race & Culture, in Race, Science & Society
Levi - Strauss C. 1965,	In Race, Science & Society. Race and History.
Mathew H.F. 1927,	Aro Sub tribes, National Archives, Enugu, Nigeria.
Meek C.K 1937,	Law & Authority in a Nigerian Tribe; London, Oxford University Press
Northcote T. 1913,	Anthropological Report on the Ibo Speaking People of Nigeria. Part 1, London, Harrison & sons.
Nwabueze B. 1985,	The Igbo in the Contest of Modern Government And Politics in Nigeria, Owerri, Ministry of Information.
Nzimiro F.I. 1962,	Political system of the Ibo, African Notes Ibadan.
Obiechina E. 1979,	The Human Dimension of History in "Arrow Of God" perspectives on Chinua Achebe, London Heinemann.
Obikwelu S.B. 1982,	Igbo-Ukwu Culture, Article.
Ofoegbu R. 1960,	An introductory treatise on the Kingship systems of Igbo people. Unpublished Mimeograph Nsukka. 1960.
Oguejiofor J.O 1996,	Influence of Igbo Traditional Religion on the socio-political Character of the Igbo. Fulladu Publishing Company, Nsukka.
Oliver R. 1961,	The Dawn of African History. Oxford University Press, London.
Onwubiko O. 1991,	African Thoughts, Religion and Culture, Enugu, Bigard Memorial Seminary.
Onwuejeogwu M.A. 1975,	Igbo Language and Culture, Ibadan, Oxford University Press,

Onwuejeogwu M.A. 1976, The Traditional Political system Of Ibusa (Ibadan, An Occasional Publication of Odinani Museum Nri, Number one.

Onwuejeogwu M.A. 1972, Odinani 1, The dawn of Igbo Civilization

Onwuejeogwu M.A 1981, An Igbo Civilization, Nri Kingdom and Hegemony, London, Ethnographical Ltd

Shakespeare W. 1970, Hamlet, Longman Group Ltd. London

Shaw T. 1970, Igbo-Ukwu, London.

Shaw T. 1977, Unearthing Igbo-Ukwu, Oxford University Press, Ibadan.

Stride G.T & Ifeka C. 1977, People and Empires of West Africa, Thomas Middlesex Thomas Nelson and sons Ltd

Talbot P.A 1926, The People of Southern Nigeria, Oxford, London.

Taylor A.J.P. 1964, The origin of the second World War, Penguine Books Ltd, Harmondsworth Middlesex England.

Ward W.E.T. 1963, A History of Africa, George Allen & Unwin Ltd.

Uchendu V.C 1965, The Igbo Of South East Nigeria, New York, Holt, Richard and Winston.

Glossary

Abigbo	A town in Igbo culture atimes village name
Adama	Ezenri's ritual Priest – usually goes with the Ezenri.
Afo	The third market day within the four market days in Igbo culture
Agballa	A divine oracle, popular in Igboland and situated in Awka. Also mentioned in Things Fall Apart
Agbaenu	Igbo area on the escapement in the Northern Igbo Plateau and the people living on his area. Sometimes a flexible concept with subtle meaning
Agbai	Traylike basket used in carrying farm produce or market items
Aguluzigbo	A town in Igbo culture, situated between Agulu and Igbo-ukwu in Agbaenu area.
Akukalia	A character in Arrow of God, sent by Umuaro as emissary to Okperi, the event that sparked off the fracas between the two communities.
Ala	The mother earth. Generally seen as the Chief administrator of human society as far as morality is concerned.
Alo	One of the ritual symbols of Eri
Ama	A form of Ozo, Igbo title used mainly in Nsukka area.

Ama-ala or Oha Obodo – A general council of all citizens

Amadioha	A divine oracle, popular in Igboland and is situated in Ozuzu
Amaigbo	An area in Orlu Local Government Area, known to have fathered many of the community of southern Igbo. Is located at the Southern edge of Agbaenu area.

Amaiyi	A designation or name for a group of communities scattered around Agbaenu
Anigbo	A Community name in Igbo culture, meaning land of the Igbo
Aro	A name of an Igbo group, that had a powerful influence around Igboland within the 18th century. Also used for lineages of the people scattered around Igboland.
Aro-Oke-Igbo	Meaning Aro people living along the boundary of Igboland. Also called Arochukwu. This place is known as the traditional home of the Aro people.
Avo	The father of Ora-eri and the founder of the town
Azigbo	A small community located adjacent to Igbo-Ukwu
Chi	Personal guardian angel or a personal God.
Chukwu	The great God. The Almighty God.
Dim	Another form of Ozo, Igbo title used around Agbaenu area and beyond
Dunukofia	A lineage, also scattered all over Igboland, but with home found in Dunukofia Local Government Area of Anambra State
Egwugwu	A masquerade cult. Represents the highest or final court of appeal in Umuofia of Things Fall Apart. A structure in Igbo societies.
Eke	The first market day in Igbo culture.
Enugwu	The top of a hill usually a designation for people or towns located on hills or highlands
Eri	The epical founder/father of Umueri kindred

Eru	A deity or divine oracle, in Things Fall Apart, found also in some Igbo communities like Nnewi.
Eze	King or leader; The Igbo word for Chief.
Ezearo	Chief of the Aro or king of the Aro people
Ezechima	A designation for the founder of Umuezechima communities could also mean chief Chima.
Ezeman	The Chief
Ezenri	The king of the nri people
Ezeofuani	The first king of the place
Ezeulu	The chief priest of Ulu – The protagonist in Arrow of God.
Ezi	Way, way to
Ezigbo	Way to Igboland
Eziowelle	A designation for Igbo communities or villages also meaning way to owelle.
Ibili –	Beads
Ibini – Ukpabi –	The long juju – A popular oracle in Igbo culture situated in Arochukwu. Famous all through Igboland
Ichi –	Traditional facial mark of the Igbo people, usually very painful blood bond taken by virile people
Ichie	Title, a form of Ozo or a bigger kind of Ozo title
Idemili	Divine oracle, with the totem as the sacred python situated in Obosi and owns the Idemili river.
Ifite	A village section in Igbo culture
Igba-Izu	Council taking
Igbo-ama-eze-	Igbo know no kings, an expression of the reality of Igbo individualism.
Igbo-bu-Igbo	The Igbo that are Igbo – and expression of chauvinism usually used by agbaenu people

	to affirm their distinctive quality among other Igbo people
Igbodo	A town in Igbo culture
Igbo-eiti	A town situated in Nsukka meaning Igbo people located in between
Igbo-eze	Also a town in Igbo culture located in Nsukka, meaning the kingly Igbo
Igbokenyi	A town in Igbo culture meaning Igbo is bigger than the elephant
Igbo-Uzo now Ibusa	Meaning Igbo people living along the way. A town or communities located on the West of the River Niger
Igwekeala	An oracle, also popular in Igboland and is situated in Umunnoha
Ikenga	The ram good in Igbo culture, also a designation for towns and villages in Igbo culture.
Ite-otu	A ceramic calabash or jar usually used for storing palm wine.
Iruigbo	A designation for some communities or villages in Igbo culture
Iruowelle	A designation for some Igbo communities or villages
Izu	Igbo week, made up of four market days, Nkwo, Eke, Oyie, Afo
Mbaise	A lineage in Igbo culture, located mainly in Imo State
Mbanese	A lineage in Igbo culture living along the Agbaenu axis.
Ndi Agbaenu	People of Agbaenu – see Agbaenu people in the text
Ndi Agbo, Ndi mba mmiri	Igbo people living on low lands or riverine areas.
Ndi Okaikpe	Lawyers
Ndi Osiali	Witnesses

Nkwo	The last of the four market days in Igbo culture
Nri	A lineage in Igbo culture, with a very influential theocracy, appeared to be nurtured in the Anambra River valley and penetrated the hinterland from this place. Also the name of a town in Anambra in Aniocha Local Government Area
Nsekpe	A dwarf that accompanies the Ezenri of Ora-eri
Nwaka	The antagonist in Arrow of god, the wealthy noble of Umunneora village
Nwandibi	A fortune teller or a shoot sayer in the Igbo culture
Nwata-ona	The bronze pectoral mask pendant worn around the neck by the Ezenri of ora-eri
Nze	Another form of Ozo title in Igbo culture
Obi	Another form of Ozo title and sometimes used to designate a king in some places
Obierika	A character in Things Fall Apart – The best friend and closest ally of Okonkwo, the protagonist.
Obika	A character in Arrow of God, the most beloved son of Ezeulu
Obigbo	The heart of Igbo or the centre of Igbo
Obi – n'etiti also Etiti	A designation for Igbo villages or sections located in between or at the center of their brother communities

Obi n'agu, also *Obiagu* or *Obeagu,* - A designation or Igbo villages or sections located near the forest zone or farm land.

Obi n'ezi agu also *Ezeagu*   A designation for Igbo villages or communities located on the route to the forest area or farm land

Obi n'ngo also *Ngo*   A designation for a village or section located on a highland or hill.

Obi n'ugbo   A designation for a section of people living near or in the farmland.

Obi n'uno   A designation for the opposite of Obi n'ugbo i.e. for the section living in the area considered to be the original home of the community.

Obi n'owelle also *Owelle*   A designation for people or community located in a place counted as off vicinity.

Ochi   A lineage in Igbo culture settled around Nnewi area

Odinani   The famous work of Michael Onwuejiogwu, also stands for culture

Ofo   One of the ritual symbols of Ezenri – The symbol of justice

Ogbe   Village section

Ogbuefi Ezeudu   A character in Things Fall Apart.

Ogwugwu   An oracle found in many Igbo communities.

Oha Obodo, also *Amaala*   General council of all citizens

Okonkwo   The protagonist in Things Fall Apart

Okpala (1)   The primus inter pares or the head of Umunna

Okpala (2)   A form of Ozo title in some Igbo cultural area

Okpalaigbo   The name of a community in Nsukka Area meaning the first born of Igbo

Okperi   A town in Arrow of God – the part setting of the book

Okpoga	Small stool used for domestic work
Oku	A clay vessel used in mixing food.
Omenala, also *Odinani* –	meaning culture or customs.
Oraeri	A small town near Igbo-Ukwu which has an Ezenri
Ora-new-eze	The king belongs to the people, an expression of the Igbo democracy
Osu	An outcast or an outlawed person
Oye	The second market day of the Igbo four market days
Ozo	A title that distinguishes the noble from the commoners. A qualification for a political appointment in the town. Usually used in the Agbaenu section
Udo	A divine oracle, found in most primitive colonies of Igbo people. Also common around Agbaenu, with one of the greatest of such in Igbo-Ukwu
Udu	A resonator in dance orchestra, also used in preserving drinking water.
Udulueze	The insignia of ritualization of the Ezenri
Ulu	A divine oracle also primitive in Igbo culture; found in Achina. Used in the work Arrow of God by Chinua Achebe.
Umu	The children of
Umuada	Women – The society of all female citizens or freeborn in a town
Umuaro	The setting of Arrow of God
Umudiana	Meaning the sons of the soil – A founding lineage of most of the Igbo communities
Umudioka	The children of dike, dike meaning the master of carving. Known as the master carving of the ichi facial mark. Found in many Igbo communities but has their traditional home in Dunukofia.

Umueri	The children of Eri – Another primitive lineage in Igbo that are also found in many Igbo communities and at times form some homogenous but very small towns.
Umueze	Literary meaning the children of the king. One of the most primitive lineage in Igbo culture, founding member of very many communities in Igboland.
Umuezechima	The children of Ezechima
Umuokotu	The children of Okotu
Umunna	Large extended or nuclear families
Umunri	Also Umueri – The children of Nri
Ume	Another version of Ozo title, common around Agbaenu
Unoka	The father of Okonkwo, the protagonist in Things Fall Apart
Uzoigbo	Way to Igbo
Uzowulu	A character in Things Fall Apart.

Index

Ike 72
Int. Major Premise 125,130
Interglacial 143
Islam 140
Isichei Elizabeth 68, 70, 73
Israelites 104
Iyase 72

J

Jaba 149
Jericho 160
Jewish Community 6,45,116
Jews 58, 134, 136, 138, 145
Jos Plateau 127
Jukun 138, 150

K

Katanga 127
Kenya 142
Kikuyu of Kenya 8
Kwa Linguistic 147, 149

L

Lamarch 34
Lead deposit 163
Levites 58, 83
Lidan 29
Lineage 8
London 106, 125
Luna Calender 139

M

Maize cob 131
Masquerade group 9, 11, 40
Mbaise 89, 92
Mediterranean shore 126,131
Mesopotamia 154
Miscegenation 35, 142
Moreo 141

Ikeji Festival 45
Ikenga 76
Isabella 45
Islamic States 24
Isoede and Esie 82
Isuofia 45, 77

Jemaa 149
Jewish Ancestry 136
Jewish Calender 140
Jewish Culture 116, 136
Judaism 140

Karmon 147
Khartoun 143, 145, 160
Kush 149

Lawyers 12
Lejja 122
Lhote 143, 144
Litigant 13
Lloyd 17
Lost wax method 110, 112

Mali 127, 142
Mauritania 127
Mbanese 90
Menelik of Ethiopia 6
Middle ages 124
Missionaries 28
Morphology 142

www.ingramcontent.com/pod-product-compliance
Lightning Source LLC
Chambersburg PA
CBHW060250290526
45789CB00001B/269